S0-AQC-599

Flow of Funds and Other Financial Concepts

Also by Jerry A. Viscione

Cases in Financial Management
Financial Analysis: Principles and Procedures
How to Construct Pro Forma Statements

Flow of Funds and Other Financial Concepts

Jerry A. Viscione, Ph.D.

National Association of Credit Management
475 Park Avenue South, New York, N.Y. 10016

Library of Congress Cataloging in Publication Data

Viscione, Jerry A.
Flow of funds and other financial concepts.

1. Financial statements. 2. Funds—flow statements.
3. Accounting. I. Title.
HF5681.B2V53   657'.48   81-2721
ISBN 0-934914-40-0   AACR2

Manufactured in the United States of America

First Printing

To Annie, Anthony, Connie, Emma, Frank, Joe, Jerry, Lou, Nellie, and Mary for being concerned relatives; Bill Bagley, Sonny La Grassa, Michael Laurano, Ralph Vertuccio (and their fine parents) for their years of friendship; the members of the Eagle Hill Civic Association for their constant encouragement and for teaching me a great deal for only three cents a point.

Contents

Tables

Flow of Funds and Other Financial Concepts

Introduction

This book is designed to enhance your ability to analyze and interpret financial statements. It does this by explaining selected principles and procedures underlying the preparation of income statements and balance sheets and by discussing the nature and scope of accounts that frequently appear on these statements.

After studying basic financial accounting principles, we will turn our attention to flow of funds analysis—the process of preparing and interpreting a statement of changes in financial position. You will find that this analysis is an essential adjunct to ratio analysis. Moreover, you will see that it does not involve much time because it is more a matter of understanding concepts than of making additional calculations. Indeed, in some cases the time required to analyze and evaluate financial statements will actually decrease.

In discussing flow of funds analysis, we will focus on the needs of external analysts in general and those of the credit manager in particular. For example, considerable space is devoted to explaining the notion of cash flow from operations and the difference between this flow and net income. Moreover, we deal with the common practice of adding depreciation expense to net income and calling the total cash flow. You will see that this sum is not cash flow at all, and in many cases it does not even come close to cash flow.

At this point a more specific outline might be helpful. The first chapter discusses the principles and procedures employed to construct income statements and balance sheets. Chapter 2 explains the nature and scope of terms, called accounts, which frequently appear on income statements and balance sheets. Although you are already familiar with much of the material covered in these chapters, I am confident that you will not only find it a useful review but that you will also see much that is new.

The third chapter covers flow of funds analysis and is followed immediately by a chapter which explores in detail the notion of cash flow from operations. The fifth and final chapter presents concluding comments and a short list of references. Finally, there are four appendices which are meant to make this booklet more useful as a reference. The first, Appendix A, is a brief glossary of accounting terms not covered in the chapters. The second, Appendix B, is a glossary of financial ratios. The third, Appendix C, contains practice problems on how to construct flow of funds statements enabling you to test and to enhance your understanding of the mechanical aspects of preparing flow of funds statements. Appendix D contains solutions to the problems in Appendix C.

I have tried to be as concise as possible and to focus on practical considerations, even if it meant short-changing important theoretical refinements. Of course, since I am an academic, I am sure that I have not been totally successful in this regard. Moreover, since we professors are the butt of many jokes that managers like to tell, I doubt that I have been completely successful in resisting the temptation to get even.

In writing this book, I received the assistance of several capable and kind people. Professor Louis Corsini, the person I go to when I have questions about financial accounting, provided numerous comments on both content and writing style. Professor George Aragon, who is my co-author on several projects, reviews most things I write. As usual his comments were constructive and he provided many creative suggestions. Professor Jeffery Ellis kindly read each chapter and was quite diplomatic in pointing out weaknesses. Ms. Barbara Holt, my research assistant, wrote the initial drafts of Appendices A and B, performed the necessary literature search, and reviewed numerous 10–K and annual reports. Ms. Mary Sullivan, the secretary of the Boston College Finance Department, did much of the editorial work and also typed the various versions of each chapter. Mr. James J. Andover, the Director of Publications for NACM, carefully reviewed each chapter and made many useful suggestions. Finally, I am solely responsible for any errors that remain.

1

Financial Accounting Concepts

In this chapter we will discuss selected topics in financial accounting which are important for financial analysis. We will explain certain assumptions, principles and procedures underlying the preparation of the two fundamental financial statements: the income statement and the balance sheet. Chapter 2 will deal with the individual items that appear on these statements.

Emphasis throughout will be on the use of accounting information by credit managers and financial analysts. We are concerned with what these people ought to know and not what accountants should know. Therefore, we will be able to avoid debits and credits, T-accounts, trial balances and similar subject areas. The accounting discipline frequently is subdivided into two catagories: managerial accounting and financial accounting. Managerial accounting refers to reports and other information prepared for the exclusive use of managers and others within the organization. Financial accounting refers to reports and data prepared primarily for external users such as stockholders, creditors, customers, employees, government bodies and other interested parties. Managers and other internal users employ financial accounting information in their work but it is the needs of the external users that are given priority when accounting principles and procedures are formulated.

Criteria for accounting principles and procedures

The purpose of accounting is to provide information which is useful for decision-making purposes. Accountants strive to supply appropriate information on a timely basis and in an understandable manner. Therefore, the fundamental criterion is: Do the principles and procedures lead to the generation of information which is useful?

Who decides which principles and procedures are to be used in writing reports? For accounting information prepared for people within the organization, the managers of that organization decide. For accounting reports prepared primarily for external users, the process is not so simple; others besides the management of the organization using the reports are involved in setting the rules. It is beyond our scope to discuss all the parties involved; we will briefly describe three: the Internal Revenue Service, the Securities and Exchange Commission, and the Financial Accounting Standards Board.

The Internal Revenue Service (IRS) was created to administer the federal tax laws. Its many duties include establishing reporting requirements for businesses. The tax rules are such that often the information required for the IRS is not suitable for other parties. For example, the income statement a firm submits to the IRS often differs from the one issued to its shareholders; both the numbers and the format differ. Thus, the amount of net income that a firm reports to the IRS often will differ from the amount reported to its stockholders. As we shall see, this practice is both reasonable and legal. At any rate, the relevant point here is that the IRS generally does not get involved in setting the rules governing the preparation and presentation of financial statements issued to investors.

The Securities and Exchange Commission (SEC) is a government agency established by the 1933 and 1934 Securities Acts. Its many duties include specifying reporting requirements for firms which sell securities (e.g., stocks and bonds) to the public. With respect to this activity, its mission is to ensure that investors receive reliable information on a timely basis. The SEC has generally, but not always, relied on the accounting profession to formulate accounting principles and procedures. The current rule-making body of the profession is the Financial Accounting Standards Board (FASB) which is an independent body whose sole purpose is to designate accounting principles and procedures. The FASB issues statements which become "generally accepted accounting principles (GAAP)." With minor exceptions, most firms must adhere to these principles in preparing reports for external use.

In the ensuing discussion we shall focus on the income statements and balance sheets that appear in a firm's annual and 10–K reports. Most of you work with these or similar statements. Those of you who work primarily with smaller companies may find that the rules are violated quite often. If so, what follows is perhaps even more important for you because it will enable you to appreciate the limitations of the statements you receive. Putting it another way, one could argue that the fact that a firm does not follow generally accepted accounting principles (GAAP) increases the risk, or at least the cost, of lending to that firm.

Accounting principles and procedures

For the remainder of the chapter we will discuss the following topics.

1. Entity Concept
2. Time Principle
3. Accounting Identity
4. Unit of Measure
5. Historical Cost Principle
6. Objectivity
7. Lower of Cost or Market Rule
8. Conservatism
9. Disclosure principle
10. Footnotes To Financials
11. Consistency Principle
12. Auditor's Opinion
13. Accrual vs. Cash Accounting
14. Realization Principle
15. Matching Principle

Two comments are in order before we proceed. First, accounting principles are not like the fundamental laws of nature; rather they were created by individuals to accomplish the goal set out above—the generation of information that is useful for decision-making purposes. Second, I referred to the above list as topics because there is some dispute with respect to which are principles, which are rules, etc. Fortunately, for our purposes such distinctions are not necessary.

An income statement and balance sheet for a hypothetical firm, the Happy Company, are shown in Table 1. An income statement presents an entity's profit performance for the period. As we shall

Table I

HAPPY COMPANY
Income Statement
For Year Ending December 31, 19X8

Net sales	$100,000
Cost of goods sold	60,000
Gross profit	$40,000
Selling, general and administrative	10,000
Interest expense	2,000
Profit before taxes	$28,000
Income tax expense	5,000
Net income	$23,000

HAPPY COMPANY
Balance Sheet
As of December 31, 19X8

Cash	$4,000	Accounts payable—trade	$3,000
Accounts receivable—net	5,000	Short-term debt	2,000
Inventory	7,000	Total current	$5,000
Total current	$16,000	Long-term debt	1,000
Fixed assets—net	23,000	Common stock	3,000
Total assets	$39,000	Paid-in capital	18,000
		Retained earnings	12,000
		Total Liabilities and owners' equity	$39,000

see, an overriding consideration in the selection of accounting procedures is to choose those which best show the results of operations, that is, the measurement of net income for a specific period of time. A balance sheet is a report which displays an entity's assets, liabilities, and owners' equity at a specific point in time.

Each statement begins with the name of the organization. This illustrates the entity concept which means that financial data are measured and reported for a specific entity, separate and apart from its owners. It can be for a business, a hospital, an organization like the National Association of Credit Management or any other unit for which it makes sense to gather economic data. For the remainder of the discussion we will refer only to the business entity.

The next line on each statement shows the time principle. Income statements always relate to a specific period of time. Although any interval is possible, monthly, quarterly, and annual income statements are most common. In contrast, a balance sheet relates to a specific point in time. This statement lists a firm's assets, liabilities and owners' equity at a certain date. Assets represent economic resources owned by the firm. Liabilities are obligations of the firm. Owners' equity represents what the owners have invested and the profits retained in the business. An alternative description is that owners' equity equals the excess of assets over liabilities. Therefore, by definition we have the following accounting identity:

Assets = Liabilities + Owners' Equity

Bookkeeping systems are designed so that this equality will be maintained at all times.

Each item on the statements is stated in terms of dollars, illustrating the unit of measure notion. This practice allows us to raise two problems. The first is: How do we account for the fact that the value of the dollar changes? For example, if the firm has the same amount of cash today as it had two years ago, this cash has less purchasing power because of inflation. The second problem is a related one: How do we account for the fact that the prices of individual assets may change? For example, if the firm owns inventory, inflation and/or other factors can cause the market value of the inventory to vary.

The answers to these questions are that we do not account for changes in the purchasing power of the dollar or for changes in the market values of individual assets. Existing practice is to rely on the historical cost principle which means that transactions are recorded at cost and maintained at this amount on the company's books. In other words, income statement and balance sheet amounts are not adjusted for variations in the general price level or for changes in the market value of individual assets.

A major reason for relying on the historical cost principle is the notion that accounting reports, to the extent possible or feasible, should be based on factual data rather than estimates. This is known as the objectivity principle. Recording transactions at cost is easy to verify, avoids any bias the preparer might possess and produces the same outcome no matter who the accountant is. However, as we shall see later, the goal of objectivity is not always achieved because in some instance estimates and/or subjective judgments are necessary or desirable.

We said above that we do not account for changes in market value of specific assets. That was not an exact statement because decreases in market value sometimes are recorded. For example, suppose a firm purchases a marketable security for $10,000 and the market price subsequently drops to $5,000. It is likely that it would be shown on the statement at $5,000 instead of $10,000. This is known as an application of the lower of cost or market rule. This rule which generally applies only to inventory and investments states that if the market value or replacement value of an asset is lower than the original cost of the asset, the lower amount should be shown.

The rationale for showing value reduction, is the notion of conservatism. This standard provides the following guidance for the accountant: When reasonable evidence exists for alternative measurements, select the one that will have the least optimistic effect on profit and financial condition.

Many accountants and other users of financial statements argue that there should be further departures from the historical cost principle. It is beyond our scope to delve into the issue and we can only mention two points. First, the opponents of historical cost thus far have been successful in winning the requirement that certain firms must present supplementary data showing the effects of general price level changes and the changes in replacement values of specific assets on their financial statements. Second and more important for our purposes, these people have shown that because of historical cost it is possible for a firm to report increasing net income numbers when its true profitability is deteriorating.

This issue raises the disclosure principle which states that information required for a fair presentation of the firm's financial position must be provided. If the information cannot be included on the statement, it must be contained in the supplementary materials. When analyzing a firm's financial performance and position, one frequently obtains the most perceptive insights by examining the information accompanying the financial statements. Footnotes which typically accompany financial statements are quite useful in this regard. For example, the balance sheet of the Happy Company shown in Table 1 includes long-term debt. When must the debt be repaid? What are important provisions of the loan? The footnotes accompanying the financials will answer questions of this nature.

In general, footnotes to financial statements contain two types of information. The first is a brief explanation of the accounting principles and procedures used in constructing the statements. The second is relevant information which cannot be included in the statements themselves. While footnotes contain much useful information, most people find them quite tedious and consider them to be a sure cure for insomnia. Many of these people who do not suffer from insomnia, simply ignore the footnotes. Unfortunately, footnotes are just too important to ignore and you will just have to bear with them.

A problem that accountants frequently encounter is what information to disclose. They cannot disclose everything; if they did, reports would be too costly and perhaps useless because of the information overload. In making this judgment they rely on the principle of materiality which means that one does not have to deal with unimportant matters. Thus, certain facts can be omitted and in some cases accounting principles can be violated if this treatment does not have a significant effect on the firm's financial condition. For example, as we shall see later, if a firm purchases an item which helps generate revenues for more than one period, it should be capitalized (i.e., recorded as an asset), and expensed over the periods during which it will provide service. For relatively small dollar amounts, accountants will not bother to capitalize them; instead they will expense the item in the period that it is acquired.

The above discussion enables us to raise a problem that we will discuss in depth later. It is that there are certain types of events for which more than one accounting treatment is acceptable. In theory at least, the preparer should select the principle which most clearly reports periodic net income. In practice, whether selection is based on the fairest or the highest level of net income is an interesting issue. At any rate, the variety of acceptable methods makes financial statement analysis more difficult. A key element in analyzing a firm's financial status is: (1) to make comparisons of the firm's progress over time; and (2) to make comparisons to similar companies. Because different accounting approaches are acceptable, comparisons among firms can be quite difficult, if not impossible. Two firms can experience identical economic events and still show very different revenue and expense numbers. With respect to comparisons over time, we can face the same problem in that the same firm can face identical economic events in two different years and report very different revenue and expense numbers each year. Fortunately, in this latter case, we are helped by the consistency principle which states that once a particular method is adopted it should be maintained. If a firm wishes to change an accounting method, it may do so but it must disclose the effect of the change on reported results.

Before proceeding with principles, it might be useful to discuss the auditor's opinion. Firms whose securities are publicly traded on the stock exchanges are required to have their financial statements audited by independent accountants. Even firms whose shares are not traded might be required by creditors or decide on their own to have an audit. A major purpose of an audit is to judge whether the firm's financial statements were prepared in accordance with generally accepted accounting principles (GAAP). The auditor will issue an opinion which is included in the firm's report. If GAAP was not followed, it will be mentioned in the opinion. Also, if there was a change from one acceptable accounting method to another, this will also be noted in the opinion along with the dollar effect the change had on reported results.

When mention is made in the opinion of a departure from GAAP or some other matter, this is called an exception or a qualification (versus the auditor issuing a "clean opinion"). Many analysts begin an evaluation by reading the auditor's opinion. If there is a qualification, it is considered a red flag and they are extra careful in conducting the analysis. (Many analysts also consider a firm's changing of auditors to be a red flag.)

We have three more topics to discuss: accrual accounting versus cash accounting, the realization principle and the matching principle. After briefly explaining the first item, we will describe the last two. We will spend more time on these last two than on any of the other topics because it is essential to have a firm grasp of them to understand financial accounting.

Accrual accounting vs cash accounting

According to the cash basis of accounting, revenues are recorded when the cash is received, and expenses are recorded when payment for them is made. Under the accrual basis of accounting, revenues are recognized and recorded when they are earned, provided that receipt is reasonably assured; expenses are recognized and recorded when they are incurred. (The precise meaning of earning revenue and incurring expenses will become clear when we discuss the realization and matching principles.) Accrual accounting provides the foundation of generally accepted accounting principles (GAAP). It is the preferred method because it provides a better measurement of a firm's profit performance and its financial condition.

Because of the use of accrual accounting, there is a difference between net income and cash flow. The amount of net income that a firm generates during a period normally will be different from the amount of cash that it generates during the same period. And very often the difference will be substantial.

Realization principle

The realization principle states that revenues should be recognized and recorded when the earning process is virtually completed, that is, when the product is sold or the service is rendered. Cash might be received at the time of sale, prior to the sale, or in a subsequent period. The amount of revenue to record is the amount of cash that has been received or that will be received in the future. Let's look at some examples.

1. The Hip Company is a retailer of men's suits. It sold $1,000 of merchandise to a customer in December on terms of net 30 days, which means the customer will pay during January. According to the realization principle, the $1,000 is recorded as revenue during December, not in January. (The cash basis of accounting would record the revenue in January when cash is received.) The rationale is that the earning process is completed during December. That is, the customer has received the product and the Hip Company has the right to collect cash. This is an asset.
2. A publisher sells a three year subscription to its monthly magazine for $90 on January 1, 19X1. The first issue is sent on January 1, 19X1, which is also the date that the publisher receives the $90. In this case $30 would be recorded as revenue each year for three years (or $2.50 per month). The rationale is that the revenue is not earned until the magazine is sent to the subscriber. If, for some reason, the firm cannot supply the magazine the customer is due a refund.
3. In late March, Joe Holt made an appointment to receive a $10 dancing lesson on April 2. He received the lesson on April 2 and paid for it the same day. The firm would record the revenue of $10 on April 2 when the lesson is given. The logic of waiting until April 2 instead of recording it at the end of March is that the earning process is not completed until the lesson is given. (The number of appointments a studio has might be relevant to readers and might be disclosed as supplementary information on a financial report. We frequently see this type of information, listed as orders received or backlog for certain types of manufacturers.)

The above examples reveal the three basic situations—cash received subsequent to, prior to and at the time of sale. For uncomplicated transactions like these, applying the realization principle is straightforward. For situations that are more complex, application is more difficult. We will explain two of these—installment sales and construction projects.

Installment sales normally represent high priced items, like a refrigerator, for which payment is made over several years. In some instances, accountants recognize the revenue when cash is received rather than at the time of sale. Is this practice consistent with the realization principle? The answer is, it depends. The realization principle says that revenue is recognized when the earning process is completed. Obviously, the process is completed when the product is sold. However, the realization principle also states that one should record the amount that is expected to be received. Thus, if there is considerable doubt as to full payment being made, then the installment method is appropriate and consistent with the realization principle. The problem is that it is normally a judgment call and different accountants might record the same transaction differently.

Actually, the installment method is not common in preparing financial statements. However, it does point out the importance of judgment in financial accounting. Moreover, as we shall see, it is a common method for tax purposes and thus has important implications for analyzing a firm's financial statements.

Another complex situation is a construction project that takes more than one accounting period to complete. For example, suppose a firm receives a contract to build a structure for $6 million. It is estimated that it will take three years to complete the project. When is the earning process completed? Some would argue when the project is completed, while others would argue that it is inappropriate to recognize all the revenue in one year since only a portion of the work will have been performed during that year. Two methods are acceptable for financial reporting. One is the completed contract method which records all the revenue when the project is finished. The second is the percentage completion method which records a portion of the total revenue each year that work is performed.

Long-term construction projects illustrate a problem mentioned earlier: there is more than one acceptable method for the same transaction. Thus, financial statement analysis is made more difficult and some standard techniques can be misleading. For example, creditors typically calculate financial ratios and then look at the industry averages. If various accounting procedures are common within the industry, such comparisons may be misleading.

To summarize, the basic principle is that revenue is recognized when the product is sold or the service is rendered, that is, when the earning process is completed. For some types of situations the application of the principle is straightforward, while for others, it is more complex. For our purposes two points are worth emphasizing. First, since various accounting treatments for the same transaction are possible, comparisons are often difficult. Second, the amount of revenue that is reported is not necessarily a good indication of how much cash has flowed into the firm.

Matching principle

The matching principle is concerned with the recording of expenses. It states that expenses incurred to generate revenue should be recorded in the same period that the revenue is recorded. We will first discuss cost of goods sold and then consider other expenses.

Cost of goods sold expense is the cost of the products or services sold during the period. The composition of the account will vary depending on the type of firm. For a manufacturing firm, cost of goods sold includes the cost of the labor, materials and overhead used to produce the products that were sold during the period. For firms that purchase and resell a product, which we will call merchandising firms, cost of goods sold expense consists of the cost of the purchased products that were sold during the period. To show the difference and the application of the matching principle, we will rely on the first three examples used to explain the realization principle.

The first example was the Hip Company which sold $1,000 of suits during December on terms of net 30 days. Suppose the firm purchased the suits from a manufacturer for $700. The $700 would be recorded as an expense in December, the same month that the sale was recorded. What if the firm purchased the suits in November? The cost would be recorded as an asset, called inventory, and then the asset would be eliminated and recorded as an expense when the suits were sold. Note that the asset would be recognized as an expense in December regardless when payment for the suits was made; payment might have occurred prior to December, in December, or in a subsequent month.

The rationale is that to measure the profitability of the $1,000 sale, we must record the costs incurred in generating the sale in the same period that the revenue is recorded. For example, suppose the Hip Company purchased the suits for $700 cash in November, sold them for $1,000 in December and collected the cash in January. There were no other costs or transactions of any nature. If we employed the cash basis of accounting, the monthly statements would be as follows:

	November	December	January
Revenues	$ 0	$ 0	$1,000
Expenses	700	0	0
Profit	($700)	0	$1,000

These statements show that November was a bad month, nothing happened in December, and January was a good month. Actually, the firm sold suits for $1,000 in December and made a profit of $300 on the transaction. Only by adhering to the realization principle would we know that the revenue was earned in December and only by following the matching principle would we know that the profit on the transaction was $300 as shown below.

	November	December	January
Revenues	$ 0	$1,000	$ 0
Expenses	$ 0	700	$ 0
Profit	$ 0	$ 300	$ 0

The second example concerned a publisher who sold a three-year subscription to its monthly magazine for $90 on January 1, 19X1 and sent the first issue to the subscriber on January 1, 19X1. For the month of January, revenue of $2.50 would be earned and hence recorded. Suppose the magazine was produced during December. The firm would have incurred materials, labor and overhead costs during December. These costs would have been recorded as an asset, called inventory, and then the asset would have been eliminated and recorded as an expense during January when the revenue was recorded. This treatment is appropriate because our goal is to measure the profitability of the $2.50 sale.

The final example concerned Joe Holt who purchased a dancing lesson for $10 on April 2—a cash sale. Suppose the person who gave the lesson was paid $5 but payment to this person was not made until May. The $5 would be recorded as an expense in April, the same month that the sale was recorded. But the firm didn't pay the dance instructor until May? In terms of measuring the profitability of the sale, it does not matter. Moreover, in April the firm incurred a legal obligation to make the payment and this obligation would be recognized by recording a liability of $5.

See if you can apply the matching principle to the following example. The Hassa Company incurs material, labor and overhead costs of $450 to produce a refrigerator which it sells to Joe Shaki for $600, payable in three equal annual installments of $200. Because of Shaki's poor credit rating, the firm decides to use the installment method and recognize revenues of $200 per year. How would the costs of $450 incurred in manufacturing the refrigerator be treated? One third of the total cost, $150, would be recorded as an expense each year.

With respect to other expenses, some are matched with sales in the same manner as cost of goods sold expense. For example, commissions based on sales are recorded as expenses in the same period that sales are recorded. There are some expenses, however, that are incurred to generate sales but are not matched to sales because it is not feasible or possible to do so. Examples are the president's salary, office supplies used in the accounting department, and interest on debt. These types of expenses are called period expenses because they are incurred with the passage of time. Thus they are matched with the period rather than with sales.

Recognizing that matching with the period rather than sales is due largely to practicality will help to avoid confusion when we see different treatments for the same type of costs. For example, suppose we start a manufacturing firm and hire two people, one to be the firm's credit manager and one to produce the products we manufacture. Both employees are paid a fixed salary. The credit manager's salary would be a period cost. The production worker's salary would be part of the product's cost which first becomes an asset and then an expense when the product is sold. The reason for the dual treatment is that it is feasible to match the production worker's salary directly to sales, but most likely this is not the case for the credit manager's salary.

Certain categories of expenses will be matched with the period in one firm and with sales in another, depending on whether the firm is involved in manufacturing activities. For example, heat, light and power would always be treated as a period cost in a merchandising firm, but a portion of these costs would be treated as product costs in a manufacturing firm.

To summarize, the matching principle states that costs incurred to generate sales should be recorded as expenses in the same period that the revenues are recorded. This is done to measure the profitability of the sales during the period, a primary goal of financial accounting. It is not feasible, however, to match all costs directly with sales and thus some are matched with the period.

Concluding comments

The purpose of this chapter was to explain selected principles and procedures underlying the preparation and reporting of financial statements. The focus on the income statement illustrates the point that an overriding consideration in the selection of accounting procedures is to pick those that provide the best measure of net income for the period. Net income measures how much the owners' equity—that is, the difference between assets and liabilities of the firm has increased because of operations.

It was shown that the realization and matching principles form the foundation of accrual accounting. Under this approach, revenues represent increases in assets and expenses represent decreases in assets. Cash is only one of many assets and that is why the cash basis of accounting is rejected.

As a creditor you are certainly interested in your customer's cash position and later we will deal with measuring cash flow from operations. For now, we must emphasize that net income and cash flow are not the same thing and very often they will be quite different. Since our customers pay us with cash, why should we care about net income?

Certainly the pattern of cash inflows and outflows is extremely important; if a firm's cash flows are not properly managed, it will certainly fail. However, if revenues are not greater than expenses by a sufficient margin, the firm is simply uneconomic and cannot survive. Putting the point another way, if a firm is not sufficiently profitable, eventually its cash inflows will not be large enough to cover its cash outflows. Unfortunately, we have seen, and will see further in the next chapter, that many difficulties can arise in applying accounting principles and thus the net income figure that the accountant reports does not necessarily provide the desired information regarding the firm's economic viability and potential.

2

Income Statement and Balance Sheet Accounts

Now that we have completed our discussion of principles and procedures of financial accounting, we are ready to tackle individual items, called accounts, which appear on income statements and balance sheets.

We shall elaborate on some of the principles and procedures covered in Chapter 1, continuing to focus on those aspects of each topic that are important for financial analysis. Our approach will continue to be to satisfy the needs of users of financial statements, not the preparers.

We won't be able to explain all the accounts that appear on income statements and balance sheets. However, Appendix A presents a glossary of selected terms not covered in this chapter. We hope that it will make this book a more useful reference.

As a basis for discussion we shall rely on the income statement and balance sheet of Isto, Inc., a hypothetical company, which are presented in Table II. We will begin with the income statement.

Table II

ISTO, INC.
Income Statement
For Year Ending December 31, 19X1

Gross sales	$160,000	
Less: sales returns and allowances	16,000	
Net sales		$144,000
Cost of goods sold		63,000
Gross margin		$ 81,000
Selling, general, and administrative expenses		42,000
Depreciation expense		4,000
Income from operations		$ 35,000
Interest expense—net		5,000
Income before taxes and extraordinary items		$ 30,000
Income taxes on operations		8,000
Income before extraordinary items		$ 22,000
Loss from fire, net of tax of $4,000		6,000
Net income		$ 16,000
Earnings per share		$ 1.30
Dividends per share		$ .60

ISTO, INC.
Balance Sheet
As of December 31, 19X1

Current Assets		*Current Liabilities*	
Cash	$ 5,000	Accounts payable	$10,000
Marketable securites, at cost		Accrued expenses	5,000
(approximate market)	8,000	Short-term debt	4,000
Accounts receivable, less		Current portion of long-	
allowance for doubtful		term debt	9,000
accounts of $200	12,000	Deferred taxes	1,000
Inventory	16,000	Total current	$29,000
Prepaid expenses	2,000	Long-term debt	19,000
Other	2,000	Deferred revenue	4,000
Total current	$45,000	Deferred taxes	7,000
Property, plant, and		Total liabilities	$59,000
equipment—net	20,000	Shareholders' equity:	
Investments	8,000	Common stock	$ 1,000
Notes receivable	6,000	Paid in capital	9,000
Goodwill	9,000	Retained earnings	22,000
Other noncurrent	3,000	Total shareholders' equity	$32,000
Total assets	$91,000	Total liabilities and	
		shareholders' equity	$91,000

Income statement

In the last chapter we explained that the purpose of an income statement is to measure the results of operations for a specific period of time. It does this by presenting revenues and expenses for the period. Revenues are defined as inflows of assets to the firm; expenses represent outflows of assets or the using up of assets owned by the firm.

Sales

The first account is gross sales which represent the total amount of goods or services sold by the firm during the period. One or two items are deducted from gross sales to compute the net amount. They are sales returns and allowances and sales discounts.

If a customer is not pleased with the product, he or she might return it and obtain a cash refund or a credit against future sales. Alternatively, the customer might be granted a price concession and pay an amount lower than the original transaction price. These types of events are called sales returns and allowances, and the total for the period is deducted from the gross sales figure.

The second item, sales discounts, is a price concession granted for payment within a specified period of time. These discounts, frequently referred to as cash discounts, are not to be confused with quantity discounts which are price concessions granted for purchasing a specified amount. These and other types of trade discounts normally do not enter accounting records.

The net sales figure represents the amount that the firm has received or expects to receive in the future. Sometimes firms include only the net sales figure on the income statement and not the other two items discussed above. When you see only the net sales figure what you know is that something has been deducted but you do not know whether it is one or two items or what the amount of each is. For example, the detail presented by Isto, Inc., indicates that most likely there are no cash discounts. However, if this detail was not presented, you probably would not be able to deduce this fact. Are firms justified in presenting only the net amount? The materiality principle discussed in the first chapter is the guide. If the amounts are significant, they should be shown on the statement.

As you know, many financial ratios include the sales figure in the computation. It is the net sales figure and not the gross sales figure that is normally used in calculating these ratios. Finally, some firms include sales returns and allowances and sales discounts among operating expenses or follow a different approach. For example, a particular firm deducts returns and allowances from gross sales to calculate net sales and treats sales discounts as an operating expense. Although the accounting treatment of these items does not affect the net income figure, it does affect certain financial ratios because the net sales figure will differ depending on the accounting method and thus it makes inter-firm comparisons more difficult.

Cost of goods sold expense

Cost of goods sold expense represents the cost of the product or services sold during the period. For a manufacturing firm, it is calculated as follows:

Beginning inventory of finished goods
+ Cost of goods manufactured
− Ending inventory of finished goods
= Cost of goods sold expense

Table III presents an illustration of a statement of cost of goods manufactured which might be included as part of the income statement, shown as a supplementary statement or not presented at all. At any rate, it is the last item on that statement, the $360,000 figure in Table III, that is part of the cost of goods sold calculation for a manufacturing firm. (Table III appears on next page.)

As we can see from Table III cost of goods manufactured includes the cost of the raw materials, labor and overhead used to produce the products during the period. A manufacturing firm will have three categories of inventories: raw materials, which are goods purchased for production but which have not yet entered the production process; work in process inventory, which includes the

TABLE III

MANUFACTURING COMPANY
Statement of Cost of Goods Manufactured
For Year Ending June 30, 19X1

Work in Process inventory beginning of period		$100,000
Raw Materials:		
Beginning inventory of raw materials	$ 40,000	
Purchases of raw materials	80,000	
Less: ending inventory of raw materials	50,000	
Raw materials used	$ 70,000	70,000
Direct labor		90,000
Overhead		150,000
Total		$410,000
Less: work in process inventory, end of period		50,000
Cost of goods manufactured		$360,000

cost of the materials, labor and overhead incurred to produce products that are not completed as of the end of the period; finished goods, which represent the cost of the raw materials, labor and overhead incurred to produce products that have been completed at the end of the period but have not yet been sold.

For a firm which does not manufacture the products it sells, the calculation is as follows:

Beginning inventory
+ Purchases
− Ending inventory
= Cost of goods sold expense

For this type of firm, there is only one inventory category.

A major complication is that goods are purchased at different prices; this issue is especially critical when the rate of inflation is high and/or changes in a dramatic fashion, or when replacement costs change due to technological change and/or demand-supply factors. To illustrate, let's suppose we start a firm which sells a single product; the product is purchased ready for sale. During the first year purchases are as follows:

Month	*Amount*	*Total Cost*
January	100 units @ $5.00	$ 500
March	200 units @ $5.50	1,100
June	200 units @ $6.00	1,200
September	200 units @ $6.50	1,300
December	300 units @ $7.00	2,100
	1,000	$6,200

At year end there are 400 units on hand indicating that 600 units were sold during the year. To calculate cost of goods sold expenses we must use the formula: beginning inventory plus purchases − ending inventory = cost of goods sold expense. Beginning inventory was zero and purchases were $6,200. What value do we place on the ending inventory of 400 units? Various costing methods are permitted. We will discuss the following three: weighted average cost; first-in, first-out (FIFO): last-in, first-out (LIFO).

The weighted average cost approach uses an average cost per unit to value the ending inventory as shown below:

$$\frac{\text{Total Dollar Cost of Inventory}}{\text{Total Units}} = \frac{\$6{,}200}{1{,}000} = \$6.20$$

Beginning inventory	$ 0
+ Purchases	6,200
− Ending inventory (400 × $6.2)	2,480
= Cost of goods sold expense	$3,720

The second method, FIFO, assumes for costing purposes that the first items purchased are the first sold. In our example the ending inventory would consist of the 300 purchased in December and 100 of September's purchases, giving an ending inventory of $2,750 and hence a cost of goods sold figure of $3,450.

The third method, LIFO, assumes for costing purposes that the last items purchased are the first sold. Thus, the ending inventory figure would include the cost of January's, March's, and one-half of June's purchases, for a total of $2,200. This amount produces a cost of goods sold figure of $4,000.

The three approaches give substantially different numbers as the following summary indicates:

	Cost of Goods Sold Expense	*Ending Inventory*
Weighted Average Cost	$3,720	$2,480
FIFO	3,450	2,750
LIFO	4,000	2,200

We can generalize from our example that when prices are rising, LIFO will give the highest cost of goods sold figure, FIFO the lowest, and the weighted average cost method an amount in between the other two approaches. As noted above, all three methods are acceptable; thus we see another instance of how varying accounting procedures can make inter-firm comparisons difficult. With respect to comparisons over time, if a firm decides to change methods it has to disclose this fact along with the dollar impact of the change on the firm's income statement and balance sheet.

In the previous chapter we saw that generally it is permissible to use one accounting procedure for tax purposes and another for financial accounting purposes. LIFO is an example of an exception. The existing tax laws require that if a firm uses LIFO for tax purposes, it must use this method for financial accounting purposes as well.[1] Since in a period of rising prices LIFO would produce the lowest tax liability (because expense would be highest under this method), why would a firm ever use FIFO? Minimizing taxes is certainly in the best interest of a firm's owners and we would certainly expect managers to minimize taxes. However, although we should be extra careful in our analysis when we see FIFO, we must not jump to conclusions because a firm might be minimizing taxes by using FIFO. For example, in the late 1970s many computer firms experienced decreasing product costs while the economy as a whole was experiencing rapid inflation.

I should note that the view expressed in the preceding paragraph represents the theoretical position that reported results do not affect stock prices. Some would aver and argue that firms use FIFO

[1]Many argue that this requirement should be changed; the issue was being considered when this chapter was written

because it maximizes reported net income which in turn has a positive effect on common stock prices.

You might have noticed that if prices are rising for a firm, the use of LIFO will produce inventory values on the balance sheet that are unrealistic; that is, the actual market value or replacement cost will be much higher than the amount reported on the balance sheet. This is an example of the problem of relying on the historical cost principle that we discussed in the previous chapter. Hopefully, supplementary data and/or accompanying footnotes would enable the reader to make reasonable judgments concerning the true value of the firm's inventory.

A major problem with LIFO is that it provides an opportunity to manipulate the net income figure. (Although manipulation is also possible with other methods, it is less likely to occur when FIFO or other methods are employed.) Managers are often expected to achieve certain profit targets. Moreover they like to show steadily increasing earnings per share figures over time. LIFO might provide these managers with an opportunity to achieve their goals. To illustrate let's assume that the firm used in the example to explain the three costing methods adopts LIFO. As noted above the firm sold 600 units the first year but purchased 1,000 units as shown below.

Month	*Amount*	*Total Cost*
January	100 units @ $5.00	$ 500
March	200 units @ $5.50	1,100
June	200 units @ $6.00	1,200
September	200 units @ $6.50	1,300
December	300 units @ $7.00	2,100
	1,000	$6,200

Let us first assume that the firm's profit performance for the year is above target. It could in December purchase 400 units instead of 300 units. The result would be a cost of goods sold expense figure of $4,100 instead of $4,000. Now suppose the firm's profit performance is worse than expected either because it anticipated selling more than 600 units or certain expenses were higher than the amount projected. It could postpone December's purchases until January. The result would be a cost of goods sold expense figure of $3,600 rather than $4,000.

As you know, cost of goods sold expense is often the most important expense for a firm which sells a product. We have just seen that the selection of the inventory costing method can have a substantial impact on the measurement of cost of goods sold expense. Thus, we observe another instance of how inter-firm comparisons can be difficult, because alternative accounting procedures are acceptable. For example, if one firm uses LIFO and another relies on FIFO, it might be a meaningless exercise to compare their profitability ratios, their liquidity ratios, and their debt ratios.

Turning to the other items, the difference between net sales and cost of goods sold expense is known as gross margin. It is also referred to as gross profit. The next account is selling, general, and administrative expenses. Selling expenses are costs incurred by the firm in its sales activities. Examples are advertising, promotion, salespersons' salaries and commissions. General and administrative expenses would include the costs of the various staff departments as well as other general business expenses.

Depreciation expense represents an allocation of the cost of a tangible asset that has a life of more than one year and that will help to generate revenues for more than one year. For example, suppose a firm purchases a machine for $5,000 which has an estimated useful life of five years and an estimated salvage value of $1,000; that is, it could be sold for $1,000 at the end of five years. It would be a violation of the matching principle to charge the entire $5,000 as an expense in the year the machine is purchased because it will help to generate revenues for five years. Therefore, a portion of the cost is allocated to each of the five years and is called depreciation expense.

We will illustrate by relying on the straight-line method which is one of several acceptable cost allocation procedures. It is computed as follows:

$$\frac{C - SV}{n} = \text{Depreciation expense per period}$$

Where:

C = Cost of asset
SV = Estimated salvage value
n = Number of periods

For our example, depreciation expense will be $800 per year as shown below:

$$\frac{\$5{,}000 \quad \$1{,}000}{5 \text{ years}} = \$800$$

Each year depreciation expense of $800 will be recorded. The asset will not be reduced by $800 each year; rather a contra-asset account, called accumulated depreciation, will be established and will be increased by $800 each year. The process for five years is:

Year	*Depreciation Expense*	*Machine*	*Accumulated Depreciation*	*Book Value*
1	$800	$5,000	$ 800	$4,200
2	800	5,000	1,600	3,400
3	800	5,000	2,400	2,600
4	800	5,000	3,200	1,800
5	800	5,000	4,000	1,000

The machine account is part of a category commonly called gross fixed assets. The difference between the machine account and its related accumulated depreciation account is known as a net fixed asset. More formally, the difference is defined as the asset's book value. It is the book value that is added to other assets to compute total assets.

As was the case with cost of goods sold expense, alternative procedures for computing depreciation expense are acceptable. Most of these are known as accelerated methods because they give higher depreciation expense figures in the earlier years of the asset's life than the straight-line method. For example, the sum-of-the-years' digits' method would produce the following stream of depreciation expense figures for the machine discussed in the above illustration.

Year	Depreciation Expense
1	1,333
2	1,067
3	800
4	533
5	267

It is beyond our scope to discuss the various depreciation methods in detail. For our purposes, it is sufficient to note that here we have another case in which inter-firm comparisons can be difficult because alternative accounting procedures are acceptable. Moreover, as we shall see later, many firms employ one depreciation method for financial accounting purposes and another for tax purposes and this dual treatment has important ramifications for financial analysis.

On the balance sheet in Table II we have an asset section called "property, plant, and equipment-net." These are the fixed asset accounts. What the firm did was to sum first all of its gross fixed asset accounts and then all of the corresponding accumulated depreciation accounts. It then subtracted the second total from the first and presented only the difference or the net amount. An alternative presentation would be the following:

Gross fixed assets
Less: accumulated depreciation
Net fixed assets

In the context of financial statements, depreciation refers simply and only to a procedure for allocating cost over time. We must stress what it does not mean.

1. It does not necessarily reflect the physical deterioration of the asset.
2. It does not necessarily indicate a decline in the asset's market value.
3. It does not imply that the firm has established a fund or intends to establish a fund to replace an asset.

Selling, general and administrative expenses and depreciation expense are subtracted from the gross margin figure to compute income from operations. This figure measures the profit performance of the firm from normal continuing operations before considering financing activities, income taxes, and unusual items. The next item, interest expense, is the cost of borrowed funds. Firms often invest surplus cash and sometimes make permanent investments. Income from these sources would be recorded here as interest and/or dividend revenue. In our example in Table 1, this type of revenue was subtracted from interest expense and only the net amount was reported.

Income tax expense

The next expense category, income tax expense, represents the income taxes that would be due based on the income reported on the income statement. The taxable income on the firm's tax return, and hence the amount actually due for the period, often will be different from the amount reported on the income statement; and the difference can be substantial. There are three basic causes: permanent differences; differences due to the carryback and carry-forward provisions of the tax laws; and timing differences.

A permanent difference arises because certain revenues are nontaxable and certain expenses are not tax deductible. An example of the former is interest on municipal securities, an example of the latter is the insurance premium paid on a life insurance policy on a firm's officer with the firm as beneficiary. The accounting impact of a permanent difference is to lower the firm's effective tax rate and it is this rate that is multiplied by taxable income on the firm's income statement.

If a firm incurs a loss, it may carry it back for three years and forward for seven years. In the case of a carryback, the firm should recognize the benefit because the refund is assured. For example, suppose a firm incurs a loss of $50,000. Because of the carryback provision it will receive a refund of $20,000. One way of presenting this information on the income statement is the following:

Operating loss	($50,000)
Income tax benefit of carryback	20,000
Net loss	($30,000)

Carryforwards are more troublesome because they depend on a firm earning income in the future. The benefit of a carryforward should not be reported on the firm's income statement unless receipt is virtually assured. Suppose in our example, the $50,000 loss occurred in the firm's first year of existence. Normally, the potential future benefit would not be recognized and the presentation would be as follows:

Operating loss	($50,000)
Income taxes	0
Net loss	($50,000)

Now suppose that although this loss was incurred in its first year, the firm had contracts with financially stable organizations that guaranteed profits of more than $50,000 in the next several years. In this situation the tax benefit of the carryforward would be recognized.

A timing difference means that the period during which the firm reports revenues and/or expenses on its income statement differs from the period when these revenues and/or expenses are reported on its tax return. Let's look at three examples.

1. A firm uses the installment method of recognizing revenue for tax purposes but reports the full sales price on its income statement. As we saw in the previous chapter, a firm should recognize the full sales price on its income statement unless there is considerable doubt with respect to payment being made. The tax laws permit the use of the installment method. Since this method would normally postpone the payment of taxes, one would expect firms to rely on it for tax purposes.
2. Accelerated methods of depreciation are allowed for tax purposes. Since they have the effect of postponing taxes, we would expect firms to rely on these methods in preparing their tax returns. Straight-line depreciation, however, might be more appropriate for the firm's income statement in the sense that it provides a better matching of revenues and expenses than an accelerated procedure. (Many firms employ straight-line depreciation for income statement purposes, but one must wonder if it

is due to accounting theory or the fact that this procedure often produces a higher earnings per share.)

3. A firm rents space in its building and receives rent for two years when the contract is signed. The entire amount is taxable in the year of receipt but for income statement purposes, the rental revenue must be spread over two years in accordance with the realization principle. Thus in this case tax expense on the income statement would be less than the amount actually paid. This difference is also reported on the balance sheet as an asset called deferred charges, prepaid taxes or some similar title.

You will more frequently encounter the type of situation described in the first two examples. To illustrate the accounting treatment, we will assume the following:

	Year 1	*Year 2*	*Year 3*
Income before taxes—income statement	$450,000	$450,000	$450,000
Taxable income—tax return	300,000	350,000	600,000
Taxes paid—assumed tax rate 50%	150,000	175,000	300,000

According to the matching principle, income tax expense will be equal to the pre-tax income shown on the income statement times the firm's effective tax rate, 50% in this illustration.

	Year 1	*Year 2*	*Year 3*
Income before taxes—income statement	$450,000	$450,000	$450,000
Income tax expense	225,000	225,000	225,000

How do we account for the difference? A liability account is established, normally called deferred taxes, and the difference is reported there. Say the deferred tax account had a zero balance at the beginning of Year 1. At the end of Year 1 it would show $75,000; it would be increased by $50,000 to $125,000 at the end of Year 2 and then decrease by $75,000 at the end of Year 3.

This accounting treatment is called a timing difference because in theory there will be a reversal as shown in the above example; that is, initially taxes paid will be less then tax expense but in a future period, Year 3 in our example, taxes paid will be larger. There are situations in the real world, however, where the reversal will not occur for a long time, if ever. To see this important point, let's look at a simple example. The facts are:

1. The Installment Company is organized to sell a product for $200 each. It sells one unit in Year 1, two units in Year 2, three units in Year 3, and three units each year thereafter.
2. Customers pay over two years, $100 per year. Since payment is virtually assured, the firm will record revenues of $200 in the year of sale.
3. For simplicity only, it will be assumed that there are no expenses other than taxes; thus, pre-tax income from each sale is $200. Finally, we will assume a tax rate of 50%.

Given the above facts we can derive the information shown in Table IV.

Table IV

INSTALLMENT COMPANY
Selected Financial Data

Year	*Pre-Tax Income Per Income Statement*	*Tax Expense*	*Taxable Income*[1]	*Taxes Paid*	*Deferred Taxes Per Balance Sheet)*
1	$200	$100	$100	$ 50	$ 50
2	400	200	300	150	100
3	600	300	500	250	150
4	600	300	600	300	150
5	600	300	600	300	150
.	.				
.		.			
.		.			
.	.	.			
infinity	600	300	600	300	150

[1] Taxable income equals cash collections from sales. In year 1, $100 is collected; in year 2 one-half of sales for years 1 and 2 are collected; in year 3 one-half of the sales for years 2 and 3 are collected. In each subsequent year collections will equal $600.

We are most concerned with deferred taxes, which are shown as a liability on the firm's balance sheet. In the first year deferred taxes amount to $50, the difference between tax expense and taxes paid. In each of the next two years deferred taxes again increase by $50. After that they do not change, for taxes paid equals tax expense. Thus, in this example, deferred taxes represent a liability which will never be paid!

To be more precise, it should be noted that taxes in each individual account will be paid but these taxes will be offset by new accounts. In other words, taxes are paid each year on part of the previous year's income but a segment of the taxes on the current year's income are postponed, automatically recreating a liability. The revolving nature of this type of liability will be explored in the next chapter.

The above example depicted a firm that stopped growing because many people rely on the following rule of thumb: growing firms should treat deferred taxes as a liability that will never be paid. Actually, a firm that is growing will show a continuously increasing liability. The only time that the deferred taxes account might be reduced is when there is a decrease in sales. Note that I said might be reduced. When sales decline, the firm might incur a loss. This, of course, would mean no income taxes would have to be paid.

In situations where it appears that the liability account might not be paid for a considerable time, if ever, many analysts adjust the firm's financial statements. They would argue that in these cases it is really a permanent difference rather than a timing difference. This, they say, would lead to a reduction in the firm's effective tax rate. The effect of this would be to increase net income, increase earnings per share, reduce the firm's deferred taxes account, and increase the firm's owners' equity. Some analysts who agree with this point of view merely treat the deferred taxes account as part of owners' equity rather than debt.

Now that I have given you the "party line," I must conclude by noting that I personally am hesitant to treat deferred taxes as an equity account. A firm can experience a decline in sales and still be profitable. In such a case deferred taxes can become a very damaging liability, especially in times when funds are desperately needed for other purposes.

The next category on the income statement is the extraordinary items section. These are events, both gains and losses, which are unusual in nature and do not occur frequently. Both conditions must be met to treat an item as extraordinary. An example would be a volcanic explosion. The extraordinary event is reported net of the tax effect. This is done because of the matching principle.

The final item on the statement is net income which is the difference between net sales and all expenses. It represents the increase in the firm's owners' equity, that is, total assets less liabilities, because of the day-to-day operations of the business.

Suppose I offered you a share of stock in one of two firms. The first has net income of $100 and the second $1,000. Both firms will earn the existing level of net income for many years into the future. Which would you choose? Your initial reaction might be to select the second. But suppose I told you that there was a total of two shares outstanding for the first firm and 1,000 for the second, that is, there are two equal owners for the first and 1,000 equal owners for the second. If you choose the first you would own $50, one-half the net income; the second would give you ownership of $1, one-thousandth of $1,000.

The above example demonstrates the importance of earnings per share (EPS). It is calculated as follows:

$$\text{EPS} = \frac{\text{Net Income} - \text{Preferred Dividends}}{\text{Weighted Number of Common Shares Outstanding}}$$

Preferred stock normally offers a fixed return that must be paid before the claims of common stockholders. Common shares outstanding refers to the number of shares owned by investors. Firms frequently purchase their own shares. These shares, known as treasury stock, may not be voted. They are not entitled to dividends, nor are they eligible for any other benefits of ownership. Since they are no longer in the hands of investors, they are not included in the number of common shares outstanding. Weighted in the formula means that an average of shares outstanding at various times in the year has been computed.

Determining the number of common shares outstanding is not a straight-forward task. There are a number of instruments and arrangements that may be used to obtain shares. Examples are convertible debt, options, and warrants. Should these potential shares be included? It is beyond our scope to delve into this issue. We will merely note that for hybrid securities, it is sometimes necessary to compute an additional earnings per share figure showing the maximum potential dilution should all instruments be converted to common stock. This second ratio is called fully diluted earnings per share. Specific rules are provided by the accounting profession for guidance in its computation.

Earnings per share does not necessarily represent the entire amount that common shareholders can receive. Because of accrual accounting, earnings per share does not represent the amount of cash flow per share generated. Moreover, even if it did represent cash flow, it is not necessarily available because the firm might need the cash to pay debt or satisfy other needs. The last item on the statement, dividends per share (DPS), indicates the amount declared for each share.

Before proceeding, we should observe that we have already referred to many of the items on the balance sheet. This illustrates the fundamental relationship between the two statements. For our purposes this means that one cannot understand and evaluate the income statement without referring to the balance sheet and vice-versa.

Balance sheet

As noted previously, a balance sheet, also known as a statement of financial position, is a listing of a firm's assets, liabilities, and owners' equity at a specific point in time. Assets are divided into two categories—current and noncurrent. A current asset is one which is either cash, or will turn into cash or be consumed within a relatively short period, normally one year. Noncurrent assets do not satisfy this criterion.

Cash represents currency on hand and deposits in banks. Marketable securities are temporary investments of cash. They normally consist of money market instruments, which are short-term debt instruments with a maturity of one year or less. In Table II the original cost of the securities was $8,000. This figure was about equal to the current market value.

Accounts receivable are amounts due to the firm from credit sales to customers. Receivables from other sources must be classified separately or lumped in with other current assets. One such example is a loan to an employee. The word net signifies that a contra-asset account, called allowance for doubtful accounts, has been subtracted from total accounts receivable. In our illustration the allowance is $200. The difference between the two accounts is called the net realizable amount. It is this quantity that is included in the calculation of total assets.

Inventory was discussed in conjunction with cost of goods sold expense. In a manufacturing firm three separate inventory accounts might be presented on the balance sheet: raw materials, work in process and finished goods. Prepaid expenses represent items which have been paid for but are not yet expenses because of the matching principle. Examples are prepaying rent and premiums on fire insurance policies. "Other" current assets are assets that meet the test of being classified as current but because of their size are not listed separately.

Turning to long-term assets, the property, plant and equipment account has already been considered in connection with our discussion of depreciation expense. We will only add here that for an asset to be included in this category it must satisfy two criteria. First it must be tangible; second, the purpose of acquiring the asset is for normal business use and not resale. For example, suppose a firm is a retailer of furniture. A desk used in this firm's accounting department would be a fixed asset, but desks on hand for sale to customers would be included in inventory. Finally, in the previous chapter, we discussed the issue of supplying readers of financial statements with information on replacement costs. For many firms the most difficult part of this process is dealing with fixed assets; market value data are not always readily available for them.

The next asset is the investments account which represents a financial commitment made by the firm with some long term or permanent objective in mind. For example, if a firm purchases shares of stock in another firm, with the intention of strengthening business ties or ultimately acquiring control of the firm, this purchase would be classified as an investment. Another example is information on subsidiaries that are not included in the consolidated statements. This aspect of financial accounting is well beyond our scope, but a few words are in order:

Many firms consist of several legal entities, a parent and subsidiaries. What we normally encounter are consolidated statements in which separate legal entities are treated as a single economic entity for financial reporting purposes. In such situations the income statement and balance sheet are consolidated to include the parent and subsidiaries. Sometimes, the consolidated statements do not include all subsidiaries. A fact that is reflected in the investments account. This often means that the consolidated statements omit significant amounts of assets and liabilities. In most of these cases, but not all, a separate balance sheet and/or income statement will be included in the annual report, burdening the reader with the problem of integrating the data.

Captive finance subsidiaries are typically not included in a firm's consolidated financial statements. A captive finance subsidiary is a wholly-owned subsidiary, established frequently by manufacturing or retailing firms, to provide wholesale financing for dealers and distributors of the parent firm's products and/or to purchase installment receivables created by retail sales of the parent's products. These captives borrow significant sums, which, as noted above, are not usually included among the liabilities of the firm's consolidated balance sheet. It would be a serious error to ignore the debt (and the assets) of the captive in performing a financial analysis. For example, many people used to consider General Motors as a firm which used relatively little, if any, long-term debt. However, its wholly-owned finance subsidiary, General Motors Acceptance Corporation (GMAC), was not included in the firm's consolidated balance sheet. GMAC's balance sheet indicated that General Motors did indeed borrow a great deal, which many people apparently chose to overlook. (Some people would quarrel with this example because General Motors, unlike many other firms with captives, is not legally liable for the debt of its finance subsidiary. While this is true, it is unlikely that General Motors would permit its subsidiary to default on its debt, making it, for all practical purposes, responsible for the debt.)

The notes receivable account represents amounts due to the firm. The word "note" signifies that there has been a written agreement. The inclusion in the noncurrent section indicates that receipt is not expected within one year from the balance sheet date.

The next category is intangibles. An intangible asset is any noncurrent asset that lacks physical substance except for financial investments which are separately classified. Goodwill is an example, and although the term has many connotations, if it appears on a balance sheet, it means the firm has paid for it. Specifically, goodwill arises when a firm acquires another firm at a price which is greater than the fair market value of the identifiable assets acquired. Goodwill, like most intangible assets, must be written off over the periods during which it helps generate revenues—the expense is called amortization. It is usually difficult to estimate the useful life of goodwill, but it must be done. The Financial Accounting Standards Board has set 40 years as the maximum period over which goodwill must be amortized.

Firms try to avoid the presence of goodwill on their balance sheets. Indeed, some people claim that merger negotiations can break down if a substantial amount of goodwill were created from the merger. The reason is that it is a drag on net income and earnings per share because it must be written off. Moreover, it is a nontax-deductible expense. (There are two methods of accounting for mergers, purchase and pooling of interests. The latter eliminates the possibility of creating in the asset column additional goodwill through the merger. The terms of the merger dictate the accounting method to be employed. The decision is not left to the firm. However, there have been cases where the terms of a merger were allegedly altered so that the desired accounting method could be employed.)

The final asset is other noncurrent which represents accounts that meet the test of being classified as noncurrent but are not separately listed because of their size. After this item, the amount of total assets is listed.

Turning to the liabilities we see that they are also divided into the categories of current and noncurrent. Current liabilities normally include those that must be eliminated within one year from the balance sheet date. Noncurrent include all obligations that do not qualify as current.

The first item is accounts payable. It can represent any short-term liability, but it usually refers to credit buying of products for resale, raw materials used in production, and supplies. Accrued expenses are expenses that have been incurred but not paid for as of the balance sheet date. Examples are payroll, income taxes due, and utilities. Short-term debt normally includes borrowings for temporary and/or seasonal financing requirements. Current portion of long-term debt is the principal portion of long-term debt due in one year. The remainder is reported as long-term debt in the noncurrent section.

Deferred taxes was discussed in the section on timing differences. Here we will only point out the difference between deferred taxes and accrued taxes. The latter is a current liability either classified separately or lumped in with other accrued expenses. Recall that deferred taxes can be a questionable liability which might never be paid. Conversely, accrued taxes represent a very real liability, one that will be paid within a relatively short period of time from the balance sheet date.

When we considered deferred taxes, we did not cover its balance sheet classification. If taxes are postponed for one year or less, it is listed as a current liability. If postponement is for more than one year, it is a noncurrent liability. If a portion is deferred for one year or less and another part is for more than a year, both accounts will appear on the balance sheet. This is the case with Isto, Inc, in Table II. The important point, however, is that the nature of the liability is the same irrespective of its balance sheet classification. Do not infer that since it appears as a current liability there is a high probability the account will be reduced. For example, in the illustration we used for the deferred taxes account that would never be reduced, (Table IV), that account would be listed as a current liability.

The deferred revenue account represents cash received but not yet earned. An example is a magazine publisher who receives payment prior to sending the magazine to the subscriber. As was explained in the last chapter, revenue received in advance is a liability because it must be returned if the firm does not deliver the good or provide the service. There is a subtle point, however, which should be explicitly stated. This is an example of a liability which is not quite the same as other liabilities. Note that the amount listed besides the account in Table II is $4,000. This figure represents the amount that has been received in advance. It does not represent the dollar amount that the firm must pay (as is the case with most liabilities). Obviously, the firm will have to expend resources to provide the goods or services, but if the sale is a profitable one, the amount will be less than $4,000.

The last segment of the statement is the stockholders' equity section, which is what the owners' equity section is frequently called when the entity is a corporation. When a corporation sells common stock, it increases the common stock account by the par value of the stock. If it sells the stock at a price above par, which is virtually always the case, it will increase the paid-in capital account for the remainder. For example, suppose a firm issues one share of stock with a par value of $1 for $20. It would increase the common stock account by $1 and increase the paid-in capital account by $19.

Par value for all practical purposes has no meaning today—stock is issued without a par value or at a price above its par value. Par value bears no relationship to market value, nor is it useful for any analytical purpose. Indeed, its only significance is to meet certain legal state statutes.

The final item is the retained earnings account which represents the portion of net income that has been reinvested in the business since its inception. Many firms have been profitable for a long time. Most of these firms will have a large retained earnings balance. However, the funds have already been invested and the account does not represent cash. As shown in Table II, the retained earning balance is $22,000. This does not mean that the firm has a pool of cash of $22,000 sitting somewhere. The $22,000 figure means simply and only that the company has retained and reinvested $22,000 of its net income since its inception. Where is the $22,000? We can't tell. It was either used to acquire assets directly or to pay off liabilities created when the assets were acquired. All we know for sure is that it is not a pool of money laying around.

How much money does the firm have? To answer this question we look to the cash account which shows a balance of $5,000.

We emphasized that the retained earnings account does not represent cash because the phrase can and does confuse many people. We should add that other items appearing on the right hand side of the balance sheet can also be confusing in this regard. Therefore, it is important to keep in mind that all the economic resources owned by the firm will always be reported as assets and will never appear in the liability or owners' equity sections of the balance sheet.

3

Flow of Funds Analysis

Now that we have completed our discussion of accounting principles, procedures and terms, we can turn our attention to flow of funds analysis.

In this chapter we will explain how to construct a flow of funds statement, introduce the concepts of net working capital and cash flow from operations, and discuss the statement of changes of financial position that many firms issue.

By flow of funds analysis, I am referring to the process of constructing and interpreting a statement of changes in financial position. This investigation makes it possible to address issues like the following.

1. What happened to net income earned during the period? Why was net income not accompanied by a similar increase in cash? As we shall see it is possible, and not uncommon, for net income to be high and for cash flow from operations to be low or negative.
2. Did the firm increase its current assets? If so, by how much, why, and was the increase properly financed?
3. Did the firm increase its fixed assets? If so, by how much, why, and was the increase properly financed?
4. Of the resources committed during the period (i. e., increases in assets), what portion was provided by the day-to-day operations of the business? What portion was financed by other sources? What were they and were they appropriate sources?
5. Was it wise for the firm to pay dividends? Where did the money come from?
6. Did operating the business during the period provide or use cash? If it provided cash, how was it employed? If it used cash, where did the needed money come from and was the source a suitable one?
7. How has the firm financed growth? Assets are needed to generate sales. To produce more sales a firm needs more assets. Higher sales, even if they are quite profitable, can create severe financial problems if they are not properly financed.

Two points raised above are quite important and deserve emphasis before we continue. The first is the notion of cash flow from operations. Because of the principles used to prepare financial statements, the firm's net income for the period normally will differ from the amount of cash produced. In some cases cash flow will be greater than net income while in others it will be less. Not only does flow of funds analysis help one investigate the difference between net income and cash flow, but as we shall see this analysis also enables one to examine another important flow, the amount of net working capital derived from operating the business.

The second point is the suitability principle which states that increases in assets should be financed with the right kind of sources. Permanent or long-term enlargements require permanent or long-term sources. Temporary or short-term increments necessitate temporary or short-term sources. For example, if I lend you $100 for one week, the increase in my receivables balance is a temporary addition because I am committing $100 for only one week. If the loan is for ten years it is a long-term increase because I am tying up my money for a long period of time. We will discuss this principle in more depth later and we shall see that flow of funds analysis aids one in evaluating whether a firm is adhering to it.

In the past one would have begun the analysis by preparing a statement of changes in financial position. Since 1971 firms have been required to include this statement in their published reports. Thus, the normal starting point now is the statement issued by the firm. Despite the change we will begin with the construction of the statement. The reason for this is that it is easier for most people to understand and apply the analysis once they know how to prepare a statement. Moreover, I suspect that a substantial number of your customers still do not issue these statements. Even if they do, the statements might cover a period different from the one you wish to study. Therefore many of you will need to know how to do it. Toward the end of the chapter we will briefly consider the statement that appears in published reports.

Before we proceed, I should mention that the statement is referred to by different names. The most frequent are the following: (1) statement of changes in financial position (most common in annual and other published reports); (2) sources and uses of funds statement; (3) flow of funds statement; (4) statement of changes in working capital. Although the world of financial statement analysis would probably be a safer place if the word funds were banned, I will use the title, flow of funds statement, to conserve space and because it is still widely-used in practice.

Preparation of a flow of funds statement

A flow of funds statement is prepared from the information provided on income statements and balance sheets. Hence the goal is not to elicit additional information, but to present the information in a more useful manner.

The statement is prepared for a specific period of time; therefore, we first select the period of interest and then obtain the income statements and balance sheets. For example, for an annual statement, we need an income statement for that year, a balance sheet as of the beginning of that year, and a balance sheet as of the end of that year. To illustrate the procedure we will construct a flow of funds statement for Year 2 for the Clinto Company. Income statements and balance sheets for years one and two are shown in Table V below:

Table V

CLINTO COMPANY
Income Statements

	Year 1	Year 2
Net sales	$2,400,000	$4,800,000
Cost of goods sold	1,920,000	3,840,000
Gross profit	$ 480,000	$ 960,000
Depreciation expense	120,000	180,000
Labor expense	240,000	480,000
Profit before taxes	$ 120,000	$ 300,000
Income taxes	60,000	150,000
Net income	$ 60,000	$ 150,000

CLINTO COMPANY
Balance Sheets

	12/31/Year 1	12/31/Year 2
Assets		
Cash	$ 30,000	$ 50,000
Accounts receivable	400,000	800,000
Inventory	160,000	320,000
Total current	$ 590,000	$1,170,000
Fixed assets—net	1,080,000	1,500,000
Total assets	$1,670,000	$2,670,000
Liabilities and equity		
Accounts payable—trade	$ 80,000	$ 160,000
Notes payable—banks	-	547,000
Accrued income taxes	12,000	30,000
Total current	$ 92,000	737,000
Deferred taxes	50,000	100,000
Common stock	190,000	300,000
Capital surplus	1,308,000	1,428,000
Retained earnings	30,000	105,000
Total liabilities and owners' equity	$1,670,000	$2,670,000

The first step is to calculate the change in each balance sheet account and label it a source or a use according to the following guide:

Source
1. Increase in a liability account
2. Increase in an owners' equity account
3. Decrease in an asset account

Use
1. Increase in an asset account
2. Decrease in a liability account
3. Decrease in an owners' equity account

Let's for a moment discuss the logic of the guide. A source means that the specific item provided the means of financing one or more of the uses. For example, if a firm issues long-term debt to finance the purchase of a building, a liability account would increase (source), as would an asset account (use). If the firm collected some of its accounts receivables and used the money to pay off a bank loan, there would be a decrease in an asset account (source), and also a decrease in a liability account (use).

Seems simple enough, so let's begin.

	At End of Year 1	*At End of Year 2*	*Change*
Cash	$30,000	$50,000	+ $20,000

There is an increase of $20,000. Cash is an asset so it is a use of $20,000. If the firm now has $20,000 more, how can we call it a use? The firm is committing to its cash account $20,000 more that had to come from somewhere. That's what a use means, and that's all it means. Why did the firm increase its cash account? Was it a good idea? We are not in a position to say. We are performing an analysis to gain insight into these issues.

We can now proceed with the first step. As noted above we first calculate the change in each balance sheet account and label it a source or a use as shown at top of next page.

After making the individual calculations, we total the sources and the uses.

Every use requires a source. The two totals must equal each

Step 1

Sources		*Uses*	
+ Accounts payable—trade	$ 80,000	+ Cash	$ 20,000
+ Notes payable—banks	547,000	+ Accounts receivable	400,000
+ Accrued income taxes	18,000	+ Inventory	160,000
+ Deferred taxes	50,000	+ Fixed assets—net	420,000
+ Common stock	110,000	Total	$1,000,000
+ Capital surplus	120,000		
+ Retained earnings	75,000		
	$1,000,000		

other. If they do not then an item was not classified correctly or there is a numerical error.

Let's pursue the exact meaning of a source and a use. Asset accounts represent uses, and liability and owners' equity accounts depict sources. The items listed above are sources and uses for Year 2. For example, at the end of Year 1 $160,000 was tied up in inventory; that is, the firm was employing $160,000 to support inventory. At the end of Year 2 $320,000 was tied up in inventory; that is, the firm was using $320,000 to support inventory at that time. The increase of $160,000 represents a use for Year 2 in the sense that this was the amount of added financing that was needed for inventory for Year 2.

We should also note that these items represent net sources and net uses for Year 2 and do not indicate how much was needed or how much was supplied for various periods within Year 2. To see this point, let us assume the following inventory balances at various times during Year 2.

12/31/Year 1	$160,000
3/31/Year 2	$ 80,000
6/30/Year 2	$580,000
9/30/Year 2	$580,000
12/31/Year 2	$320,000

As explained above, the use for Year 2 was $160,000. This figure is the net amount required for Year 2. However, we can see that for the first quarter, inventory declined from $160,000 to $80,000, making it a source for this period. From the end of the first quarter to the end of the second quarter, it was a use of $500,000. It was neither a source nor a use for the third quarter. For the fourth quarter it was a source of $260,000. We could continue and show monthly, weekly, or even daily changes. The message we'd like to get across is this: When looking at annual changes in individual items, do not infer that the amount specifies the total or the maximum inflow or outflow related to that item for the year.

Adjustments

Here are three adjustments that should make the previous statement more informative:

1. Remove the change in retained earnings and substitute net income as a source and dividends as a use. (A net loss would be a use.)
2. Show the amount of net working capital provided by operations. This is done by adding (or subtracting) certain items to net income. (As we shall see later net working capital provided by operations is frequently referred to as funds flow or funds provided by operations.)
3. Remove the change in net fixed assets and substitute the net amount spent on fixed assets.

To make these adjustments we need income statement data for Year 2.

Retained earnings adjustment

Let's look at the rule first and then learn how to apply it.

Rule
Remove the change in retained earnings and substitute net income as a source and dividends as a use.

The income statement for Year 2 indicates that net income was $150,000. Information regarding dividends is normally given on the income statement or on the statement of retained earnings. In this case we do not have a retained earnings statement, and dividends are not shown on the income statement, so we must estimate the amount.

You may recall that the two major items affecting the retained earnings account are net income and dividends. Specifically, the end of period retained earnings balance may be calculated as follows:

Retained earnings balance, beginning of period
+ Net income for period
− Dividends for the period
= Retained earnings balance, end of period.

For our example, we can use this formula to derive the amount.

Retained earnings balance, end of Year 1	$30,000
+ Net income for Year 2	150,000
− Dividends for Year 2	?
= Retained earnings balance, end of Year 2	$105,000

Since we know three of the four items in the equation, we can figure out that dividends were $75,000.

Now we can apply the rule. We remove the $75,000 change in retained earnings from the statement and substitute income of $150,000 as a source and dividends of $75,000 as a use.

Why do we make this adjustment? The answer is to make the statement contain more useful information. The change in the retained earnings account of $75,000 could be the result of literally an infinite number of combinations of net income and dividends. For example, net income of $1,075,000 and dividends of $1,000,000 would produce a change of $75,000. Whether net income and dividends were these amounts or $150,000 and $75,000 is obviously important information which cannot be gleaned by looking only at the change in retained earnings.

Before turning to the next adjustment, I should point out that although net income and dividends are usually the major items affecting the retained earnings balance, sometimes there will be others. If this is the case, the information typically will be provided on the statement of retained earnings or the income statement, where you can make the appropriate modification. (When the additional items are relatively small, many analysts ignore them and do not make further adjustments.)

Net working capital adjustment

Before stating the procedure, I should mention that the rule we will employ gives an estimate and not an exact figure. Also, I will be referring to a firm's current assets as working capital, and the difference between current assets and current liabilities as net working capital. This is the procedure used by finance people. Accountants typically do not employ a separate definition for current assets. They call the difference between current assets and current liabilities working capital.

Here's the rule:

> **Rule**
> Remove the change in the long-term deferred taxes liability from the statement. To the net income figure add an increase (or subtract a decrease) in the long-term deferred taxes account. Also, add expenses on the income statement that do not decrease net working capital.[1]

Before illustrating how to apply the rule, we should briefly explore its logic. Generally, the only source of net working capital from operating the business is revenues. Some expenses decrease net working capital, but not all expenses decrease it. In preparing a flow of funds statement we could present revenues that increase net working capital as a source and expenses that decrease it as a use. While this perhaps should be done, it is not normal practice. Instead, analysts usually adjust the net income number. Specifically, they make the following calculation:

Net Income (or Net Loss) for period
\+ Expenses that do not decrease net working capital
= Increase (or decrease) in net working capital from operations for period.

[1]To obtain a more accurate estimate, one should also subtract from net income revenues that do not increase net working capital. Moreover, it is possible to have a long-term deferred taxes asset account. If so, an increase in it would be subtracted and a decrease would be added. In most cases, these items will not exist or will be relatively small. I will not include these refinements in the discussion.

It is beyond our scope to describe all the expenses that do not decrease net working capital. However, we should mention three expenses: depreciation, amortization, and a portion of income taxes. Amortization expense and depreciation expense are simply added to the net income figure. The portion of income tax expense that does not decrease net working capital is derived by adding the increase (or subtracting the decrease) in the long-term deferred taxes account. The liability, deferred taxes, could be current or non-current and some firms have both on their balance sheets. It is only the change in the long-term liability that is involved in this calculation.

When you prepare a flow of funds statement, you will not always be able to identify all the expenses that decrease net working capital. Hence, your calculation will be an estimate, not an exact figure. However, you will normally be able to uncover the major dollar portion, allowing you to derive a good estimate. (Very often depreciation expense and the change in the long-term deferred taxes account will be the major dollar items. If the firm is in the natural resources business, depletion likely will be a major expense that does not decrease net working capital. You should be able to spot this item.)

Let's now apply the rule to the Clinto Company. We start with net income for Year 2 of $150,000. To this figure we add the $50,000 increase in the long-term deferred taxes account and depreciation expense of $180,000. The total is $380,000 as shown below:

Net income for Year 2	$150,000
Increase in long-term deferred taxes	50,000
Depreciation expense	180,000
Net working capital provided by operations for year 2	$380,000

We will discuss the significance of this quantity, the amount of net working capital provided by operations, after we complete our discussion of the construction of the statement.

Fixed asset adjustment

Firms acquire and sell fixed assets. The purpose of this adjustment is to provide information on this activity. Specifically, it gives an estimate of the net amount spent as defined below:

Amount spent on fixed assets
− Proceeds from sale of fixed assets
= Net amount spent on fixed assets

Although we would like to know both the amount spent and the proceeds from sales, generally this is not possible from income statement and balance sheet data. We must settle for information on the net amount spent. Moreover, we can only derive an estimate of the net amount spent.

More than one procedure is used for making the adjustment. The one we will rely on should give the best estimate in most instances.

Rule
Add depreciation expense for the period to the change in net fixed assets to obtain an estimate on the net amount spent on fixed assets. This derived quantity replaces the change in net fixed assets on the statement.

Applying the rule to our illustration produces an estimate of $600,000 as shown below:

Change in net fixed assets	$420,000
+ Depreciation expense for year 2	180,000
= Net amount spent on fixed assets	$600,000

Incorporating the adjustments

The final step is to incorporate the adjustments into the statement. Let us first briefly summarize them.

1. Remove the change in retained earnings of $75,000, show net income of $150,000 as a source and dividends of $75,000 as a use.
2. Show a new category, called net working capital from opera-

tions, which is equal to net income of $150,000 plus depreciation expense of $180,000 plus the increase in deferred taxes (long-term) of $50,000. The increase in the deferred taxes account is removed from the statement.

3. Remove the change in net fixed assets of $420,000 and replace it with the net amount spent on fixed assets of $600,000.

The final statement is shown in Table VI.

Table VI

CLINTO COMPANY
Flow of Funds Statement
For Year 2

Sources		
Net income	$ 150,000	
+ Depreciation expense	180,000	
+ Deferred taxes (long-term)	50,000	
Net Working Capital		$ 380,000
Notes payable—banks		547,000
Accounts payable		80,000
Accrued income taxes		18,000
Common stock		110,000
Capital surplus		120,000
		$1,255,000
Uses		
Dividends		$ 75,000
Cash		20,000
Accounts receivable		400,000
Inventory		160,000
Net amount spent on fixed assets		600,000
		$1,255,000

We will now consider further the notion of net working capital provided by operations. Following that I will explain how to calculate cash flow from operations and discuss its significance. Then we will expand on our earlier discussion of the suitability principle. It is necessary to understand these three concepts in order to evaluate properly a flow of funds statement. Before proceeding, however, I should briefly alert you to the semantic problem surrounding the use of the word funds.

Caution: The word funds could be dangerous to your financial analysis

The word funds is used a great deal in finance, accounting, and economics. Its precise meaning will depend on the context in which it is being employed. It is impossible to enumerate all the meanings that are attached to the word but some of the more common are: (1) net working capital; (2) cash; (3) cash plus marketable securities; (4) assets; (5) ability to acquire assets.

The variation in usage leads to errors in financial analysis. The following two are fairly common and are especially serious when committed by creditors.

1. We just explained how to estimate the amount of net working capital generated by operations. This quantity is frequently called funds provided by operations, funds flow, or some similar name. The error is that when it is referred to by a phrase with the word funds in it, many people interpret it as an estimate of the amount of cash produced by operating the business. The fact is that the measure does not represent cash, and very often it will be quite different from the amount of cash generated.
2. The first error has produced another that is just as serious. Many analysts add depreciation expense to net income and call it the total cash flow. Actually the sum is an estimate of the amount of net working capital provided by operations. This error is so frequently committed that it deserves more attention than we can give it here. We will explore it in more detail in the next chapter.

Net working capital from operations

In discussing the preparation of a flow funds statement, we explained how to estimate the amount of net working capital provided by operations; that is, how much day-to-day operations increased (or decreased) net working capital. We also pointed out that this estimate does not represent cash flow. If it isn't cash flow, why bother to estimate it or even think about it? After all, we can only spend cash. We cannot spend net working capital.

The concept of net working capital is important because it indicates the extent to which day-to-day operations can support a firm's financial requirements. For example, if a firm is experiencing increasing sales, net working capital will increase, requiring perhaps an expansion of fixed assets as well. If net working capital from operations is less than the needed increment in net working capital, then the remainder must be financed from another source. If the amount of net working capital generated from operations is greater than the needed addition, then the excess can be used to acquire fixed assets, to pay down loans, to pay dividends, or for some other purpose.

Net working capital from operations is a useful way of thinking about the flow of financial resources because a firm needs assets to support operations, and cash is only one of the many types of assets required. Therefore, the net amount of assets that flow into the firm from its operations is an important piece of information. But it is just as important to recognize that it does not signify the net amount of cash that has been produced.

Finally, we should note that the change in net working capital for the period normally will not equal the amount of net working capital from operations. The reason is that increases and decreases occur because of other factors. For example, if a firm issues common stock and uses the proceeds to pay down short-term debts, net working capital will increase, but this change is not due to day-to-day operations.

Cash flow from operations

Measuring and appraising the amount of cash that has been generated or used for operating the business should be an essential part of an analysis. As was pointed out earlier, it is quite possible for a firm to have positive and growing profits and at the same time to have operations consume rather than supply cash. While this is not necessarily a bad sign, especially in the case of a firm undergoing sales growth, it could be an indication of trouble, and deserves a careful diagnosis. On the other hand, positive cash flow from operations is not necessarily a sign of strength and soundness. While firms in excellent financial shape can produce positive cash flows, businesses enduring a deteriorating situation can also provide positive cash flows. For example, if sales are declining for a firm, net working capital required will normally decrease, perhaps causing cash flow from operations to be positive in spite of low or negative profits. This situation could be due to a recession, and we might conclude that there is nothing fundamentally wrong with the firm's management and that sales and profits will rebound once the economy improves. In this type of circumstance we would be concerned about the disposition of the cash because the money will be needed when sales rebound.

Looking at another scenario, sales could decline because a firm is losing market share due to its inability to be competitive. While cash flow might be positive, we certainly should not be pleased about this type of situation. Cash flow from operations is defined as follows:

Cash inflows from selling goods and services
– Cash outlays made in connection with purchasing or producing products for sale and for other expenses
= (Net) Cash flow from operations.

We can see that this definition does not include all the cash inflows and cash outflows for the period. Cash flows into the firm from other sources such as the proceeds from bond or stock issues. Cash flows leave the firm for other purposes such as acquiring fixed assets, paying debts and paying dividends. The change in the firm's cash account reflects all inflows and outflows. Therefore, examining the change in the firm's cash account does not tell us if day-to-day operations used or provided cash.

To calculate the exact amount of cash flow from operations would require an analysis of a firm's internal accounting records. From the data presented on income statements and balance sheets we can only derive an estimate. Usually it will be a good one. What we do is adjust net working capital from operations for changes in those current assets and current liabilities that vary automatically with sales. We add increases in the liability accounts and decreases in the asset accounts. We subtract decreases in the liability accounts and increases in the asset accounts. The current accounts normally included in the estimating procedure are: receivables from customers, inventory, prepaid expenses, payables to suppliers, accrued expenses and the short-term deferred taxes account.

We will illustrate the calculation by relying on the Clinto Company. First, we will summarize the rule.

Net working capital from operations for the period
± Change in accounts receivable
± Change in inventory
± Change in prepaid expenses
± Change in accounts payable—trade
± Change in accrued expenses
± Change in short-term deferred taxes
= Cash flow from operations for the period

For Clinto cash flow from operations was a negative $82,000 as shown below.

Net Working Capital from operations for Year 2	$380,000
− Increase in accounts receivable	−400,000
− Increase in inventory	−160,000
+ Increase in accounts payable	+80,000
+ Increase in accrued income taxes	+18,000
= Cash flow from operations for Year 2	−$82,000

The negative figure means that cash outflows exceeded cash inflows. (A more detailed explanation of the procedure is presented in the next chapter.)

Earlier we stressed that one must not confuse the flows of net working capital and cash from operations. Here we see that Clinto generated $380,000 of net working capital from operations during year 2 but cash flow was a negative $82,000.

Before continuing, we should note a limitation of the measure of cash flow from operations. A major purpose of this calculation is to help one evaluate if a firm is a cash generator or a cash consumer. One problem with the measure employed is that changes in the cash and fixed asset accounts normally are not included (at least not in published flow of funds statements). But these two assets also change because of sales. A firm requires a certain amount of cash to handle day-to-day transactions. If the number or size of transactions changes, then the amount of cash needed may also change. Moreover, if a firm is at or close to capacity, it will need more fixed assets to produce a higher level of sales. Thus, the cash flow from operations figure does not necessarily represent the amount of money available for purposes such as paying off loans or paying dividends. It is left to the analyst to make a judgment on this matter.

Let us pause for a moment so that you can maintain (or regain) your focus. Our purpose in this chapter is to explain how to prepare and to evaluate a flow of funds statement. Naturally, the evaluation and interpretation stage is the key, but as noted earlier one must understand certain essential concepts to perform this task properly. We have just discussed two of them, net working capital and cash flow from operations. There is one more, the suitability principle, and we will now turn our attention to it.

Suitability principle

I should begin by noting that the suitability principle is known by a variety of other names, the most common being: (1) the matching principle, (2) matching maturities of assets and liabilities, (3) appropriate financing and (4) the hedging principle. The notion itself is simple: Uses of funds should be financed with the right kind of sources. Permanent or long-term uses necessitate permanent or long-term sources. Temporary or short-term uses require temporary or short-term sources. To repeat the example cited earlier, if I lend you $100 for one week, the increase in my receivables balance is a temporary use because I am tying up $100 for only one week. If the loan is for ten years, then it is a permanent or long-term use because I am committing my money for a long period of time.

The only tricky part in applying the principle to financial statement analysis is that you cannot rely on balance sheet classifications for designation. For example, although accounts payable and accrued expenses are listed on a balance sheet as current liabilities, they are permanent sources in the sense that they are continuously recreated. To see the logic, if a firm purchases $50 each month on terms of net 30 days, its accounts payable balance will be $50 as long as monthly purchases are $50. Putting it another way, if a firm needed $50 of inventory to support operations and trade credit was not available, it would need another source; and the source should be a permanent one. (Naturally, if a firm does not pay its bills on time, the stretched portion of its payables or accrued expenses should not be viewed as a permanent source of funds.)

Looking at current assets, we noted earlier that many of them change automatically with sales. Suppose a firm sells $100 per month on terms of net 30 days, and customers pay when due. If sales increase from $100 to $200 per month, accounts receivable will increase automatically from $100 to $200. If the higher sales are temporary, the increase would be temporary indicating that a short-term source, like a short-term bank loan, is the appropriate way to finance the increment in receivables. If the higher sales are permanent, then the addition to receivables would be permanent, calling for a permanent or long-term source. Inventory and a portion of the firm's cash balance behave in the same manner. Sometimes other current assets, like prepaid expenses, also change automatically with sales.

Finally, any liability due beyond one year is usually classified as long-term on a balance sheet. It obviously makes a difference whether the debt is due in two years or 20 years. So, when analyzing a flow of funds statement, do not automatically assume that the suitability principle has been adhered to if long-term debt is the source for a long-term or permanent use.

Analyzing Clinto's flow of funds statement

We can now turn to the evaluation and interpretation of Clinto's flow of funds statement for year 2. Our primary purpose is to focus on applying the concepts discussed so far; thus, what follows should not be viewed as a comprehensive guide to analyzing flow of funds statements. (Indeed, I believe that there is no ideal guide because so much depends on the purpose of the analysis and the nature of the firm involved.)

To put the sources and uses in perspective, we should begin by looking at the sales figures for years 1 and 2. We see that sales doubled. Next our concern is whether the increase is permanent or temporary. Since we are evaluating annual statements and the closing date is the same, it is unlikely that the change in sales is due to seasonal factors. This is an important point because a frequent cause of temporary periodic variations in sales creating temporary financial requirements is seasonality. (Note that because of the seasonal factor, one must be careful when comparing balance sheets for different points during the year. Such comparisons can be misleading.)

The absence of a seasonal influence does not guarantee that the increase is permanent, especially when the rate is as large as Clinto's 100%. The analyst must look to other information to make a judgement on this issue. For example, projections of the future state of the economy and information contained in annual and 10–K reports can be quite helpful in making such a judgment. For purposes of this discussion, we will assume that our search reveals that the increase in sales is permanent; that is, we expect sales for subsequent years to be $4.8 million or more.

Next we will look at the current assets and current liabilities that change automatically with sales. In this example, these are accounts receivable, inventory, accounts payable, and accrued income taxes. The only other possible candidate here is the cash balance, but we will ignore it for now. The first issue is: Are the increases in these accounts due to sales or some other factor? As you know, ration analysis is used to provide insight into issues like this one, and it would lead us to infer that the increases in these accounts seem to be due to the higher level of sales.

Since the increase in sales is permanent, the higher receivables and inventory balance are permanent also indicating that a permanent or long-term source is required. Accounts receivables plus inventory increased by $560,000, and the automatic sources (accounts payable and accrued income taxes) increased by $98,000; therefore, the difference of $462,000 must be financed with a permanent source. Dividends and fixed assets require permanent or long-term sources. The increase in cash would also be in this category if it were due to sales.

With respect to sources, we have already noted that accounts payable and accrued income taxes increased because of sales. They can be then viewed as permanent sources. Net working capital provided by operations, common stock, and capital surplus are permanent sources. (In this example, operations provided $380,000 of total sources of $1,255,000, or 30%. In many cases, the percentage will be much larger; that is why we spent so much time discussing the concept.)

The large increase in the short-term bank debt is troublesome. All the uses are permanent and it appears that a large proportion of these was financed with a temporary source. We can't jump to conclusions, however, because the debt might be more permanent than it looks. For example, a loan arrangement based on the size of a firm's receivables might be listed as a current liability, but for all practical purposes it is a long-term loan. Nevertheless, this is a hint that something might be wrong, and it represents an area that requires further investigation.

Why are we worried? The reason is that the firm might not be able to pay the loan when it is due. The money will not come from a decrease in assets because our analysis indicated that they were permanent uses. Cash flow from operations might be negative again during year 3. Even if it is positive, it might not be large enough or flow in soon enough. What about new loans or stock issues? These might not be possible. Even if they are, it takes time to arrange these transactions and this factor could be a problem. Perhaps the most penetrating question is: How did Clinto get itself in this position in the first place? Was it incompetent management?

We can see that Clinto could face financial embarrassment or worse, despite its substantial increase in profits. Putting it another way, a violation of the suitability principle implies that a firm may be unable to meet its financial obligations when they are due.

Clinto is a hypothetical company, but there are many firms around that violate the suitability principle. One reason why firms violate it, especially small companies, is because their managers do not understand the difference among the flows of income, net working capital from operations and cash flow from operations. Whatever the reason we should inquire into what happens to these firms. Some learn right away and put their houses in order quickly, others undergo a long, painful process, and some even cease to exist as independent companies. For our purposes, it is important to note that one thing many of them do is stretch their accounts payable. That is, they do not pay you. (I wonder how many of you have paid for your customers' lesson in financial management.)

Before closing this chapter we should comment briefly on the flow of funds statement that firms include in their published reports. We will consider the statement that is included in annual reports.

Statement of changes in financial position

As noted earlier, firms are now required to include a flow of funds statement in their published reports. Often this will be the starting point of your analysis. Since we have already discussed the concepts and tools necessary to evaluate and interpret these statements, we will be discussing issues of format rather than substance.

The statement you will encounter in an annual report normally will be an annual statement. There will be two of them, one for the current year and one for the previous year. The name recommended for the statement by the accounting profession is: Statement of Changes in Financial Position. Most firms use this title but there are others. Moreover, while many firms use phrases like working capital provided by operations to describe the amount of net working capital generated by operations, some use labels like funds flows, funds and funds provided by operations. (As noted earlier what we call net working capital most accountants call working capital.)

The statement we constructed for Clinto is similar to those in annual reports prepared from income statement and balance sheet data. However, since a firm's accountants have access to more information, they can present more. For example, one of the adjustments we discussed would provide an estimate of the net amount spent on fixed assets. The statement included in annual reports will give an exact amount.

In addition, instead of seeing just the net amount spent, you will frequently run across the total amount spent listed as a use and proceeds from the sale of fixed assets as a source. Moreover, we had to settle for an estimate of net working capital from operations because we could not identify all expenses that do not decrease net working capital. This is not the case with published statements since the preparer has access to internal accounting records.

In our statement, we included the quantity net working capital from operations. Most published statements include the same quantity, but some will show cash flow from operations. The layout of the statement will probably be quite different from the one we constructed. Specifically, many firms include the following in the body of the statement: net working capital from operations, the change in each noncurrent account, and only one entry for a change in net working capital (which is usually called working capital). In other words, the changes in current assets and current liabilities will be summarized in one number, and only this number will be included in the body of the statement. If this format is followed, and it is quite common, then the change in each current asset and each current liability must be shown below the main body of the statement. To help you see the difference and similarity between this format and the approach we employed earlier, Table VII presents a flow of funds statement for Clinto for year 2 using the layout described in this paragraph.

Table VII

CLINTO COMPANY
Statement of Changes in Financial Position—Working Capital Basis
For Year 2

Resources provided:	
Working capital from operations:	
Net income	$150,000
Add: Depreciation expense	180,000
Increase in deferred taxes—noncurrent	50,000
Working capital from operations	$380,000
Common stock	110,000
Capital surplus	120,000
Total resources provided	$610,000
Resources applied	
Dividends	$ 75,000
Net amount spent on fixed assets	600,000
Total resources applied	$675,000
Decrease in working capital	$ 65,000

CLINTO COMPANY
Statement of Changes in Financial Position—Working Capital Basis
For Year 2

	Composition of Working Capital		
	End of Year 1	End of Year 2	Increase (Decrease) in Working Capital
Cash	$ 30,000	$ 50,000	$ 20,000
Accounts receivable	400,000	800,000	400,000
Inventory	160,000	320,000	160,000
Total current	$ 590,000	$1,170,000	
Accounts payable—trade	$ 80,000	$ 160,000	(80,000)
Notes payable—banks	-	547,000	(547,000)
Accrued income taxes	12,000	30,000	(18,000)
Total current	$ 92,000	$ 737,000	($ 65,000)

Concluding comments

Flow of funds analysis should be an essential part of a credit evaluation. Ratios can be quite helpful; however, they should be employed with this analysis. They are no substitute for it.

If most of your customers are small firms that are not subject to the reporting requirements of larger firms, they probably do not issue a flow of funds statement. If so, you will have to begin the analysis by preparing the statement. I suggest you perform this activity before calculating ratios. The reason is that once you become comfortable with the concepts of net working capital and cash flow from operations, you will likely want to use these quantities in the calculation on certain ratios. (For those of you who will have to prepare these statements, Appendix C at the end of the book contains problems with solutions, giving you the opportunity to practice the mechanics.)

Table VIII summarizes the procedures discussed in the chapter for estimating net working capital and cash flow from operations. It is repeated here for your convenience when you have to refer to them in the future.

Table VIII

Procedures for Estimating Net Working Capital and Cash Flow from Operations

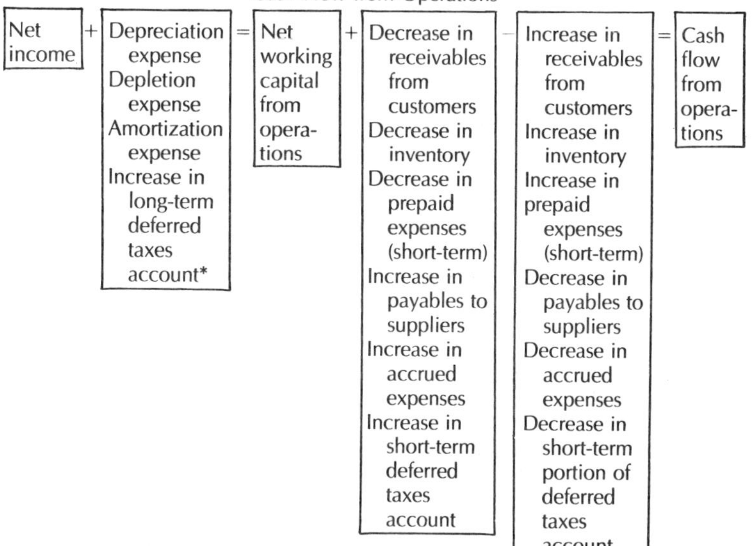

Net income	+	Depreciation expense Depletion expense Amortization expense Increase in long-term deferred taxes account*	=	Net working capital from operations	+	Decrease in receivables from customers Decrease in inventory Decrease in prepaid expenses (short-term) Increase in payables to suppliers Increase in accrued expenses Increase in short-term deferred taxes account	−	Increase in receivables from customers Increase in inventory Increase in prepaid expenses (short-term) Decrease in payables to suppliers Decrease in accrued expenses Decrease in short-term portion of deferred taxes account	=	Cash flow from operations

*subtract a decrease

4

Cash Flow from Operations

In this chapter we will discuss the concept of cash flow from operations in depth and then explain how to go about estimating it. We will also cover the widely-used method of adding depreciation expense to net income. Our aim is to get you to see the glaring faults of this method and to help you develop your ability to deal with other rules of thumb.

Let us begin by examining the logic of estimating cash flow from operations as described in Chapter 3. We will again rely on the statistics for the Clinto Company for Year 2. Please refer to the income statements, balance sheet and flow of funds statement presented in Tables V and VI on pages 65 and 73.

We defined cash flow from operations as follows:

Cash inflow from selling goods and services
− Cash outlays made in connection with purchasing or producing products for sale and for other expenses
= (Net) Cash flow from operations.

We have also estimated Clinto's cash flow from operations for Year 2 as follows:

Net working capital from operations for Year 2	$380,000
− Increase in accounts receivable	−400,000
− Increase in inventory	−160,000
+ Increase in accounts payable	+80,000
+ Increase in accrued income taxes	+18,000
= Cash flow from operations for Year 2	$−82,000

Let us now look more closely at each component of the computation. The only source of cash (or any other asset) from operations is from revenues. For Year 2 the Clinto Company had net sales of $4.8 million. However, at the end of Year 2, the receivables balance was $800,000, implying that only $4 million of the $4.8 million was collected during Year 2. What about the $400,000 accounts receivable balance at the end of Year 1? This amount most likely relates to sales for Year 1 which was collected during Year 2. Therefore, the total cash inflows from sales for Year 2 was $4.4 million. To generalize, cash inflows from sales can be calculated as follows:

Receivables (from customers) balance, beginning of period
+ Net sales for the period
− Receivables (from customers) balance, end of period
= Cash inflows from sales during the period

For Clinto

Accounts receivable, end of Year 1	$400,000
+ Net sales for Year 2	4,800,000
− Accounts receivable, end of Year 2	800,000
Cash inflows from sales during Year 2	$4,400,000

The above formula permits us to calculate cash inflows from sales without having to distinguish between cash and credit sales. Moreover, we do not have to know which sales period the receivables balance refers to. For example, the $800,000 balance at the end of Year 2 likely relates to Year 2's sales, but part of the balance could be from earlier sales. For purposes of calculating cash inflows it does not matter.

The changes in the other three accounts (inventory, accounts payable and accrued income taxes) relate to cash outlays for expenses. To understand these, it might be helpful if we briefly review the accounting concept known as the matching principle, which was explained in depth in the accounting chapters. The principle states that costs incurred to generate revenues should be recorded as expenses in the same period that the revenues are recorded irrespective of when payment for them is made. When payment for the expense is made in advance, the prepayment is shown as an asset, called prepaid expenses, deferred charges or some similar title, until the expense is recorded. When payment is made in a subsequent period, a liability (an accrued expense account) will be recorded on the balance sheet at the end of the period.

On Clinto's income statement, there are four expense categories: cost of goods sold, depreciation, labor, and income taxes. (We will discuss each, saving cost of goods sold for last.) Depreciation expense was $180,000, but this is a noncash expense. Labor expense was $480,000 for Year 2. If a portion of labor expense is normally prepaid, we would find a short-term asset relating to it. There is no such asset on Clinto's balance sheet. If a portion of it is paid subsequent to the end of the accounting period, we would find an accrued liability pertaining to it. There is only one accrued expense on Clinto's balance sheet and it relates to taxes. We can conclude, therefore, that payments for labor expense for Year 2 were $480,000.

Income tax expense for Year 2 was $150,000. The increase in deferred taxes of $50,000 indicates that only $100,000 is actually due for Year 2. To compute how much was paid during Year 2, we must scan the balance sheet to see if any prepaid items or accrued liabilities relate to income tax expense. For the Clinto Company we see that there is an accrued tax account with a balance of $30,000 at the end of Year 2, indicating that this portion of the taxes payable for Year 2 will be paid during Year 3. The end of Year 1 balance of $12,000 means that this portion of Year 1's taxes will be paid during Year 2. Thus, total payment for taxes for Year 2 was $82,000. This amount can also be calculated as follows:

Accrued taxes, end of Year 1	$12,000
+ Income taxes due for Year 2	100,000
− Accrued taxes, end of Year 2	30,000
Cash outlays for income taxes for Year 2	$82,000

This formula can be applied to other expenses besides income taxes. In fact it is more straightforward to apply the formula in such categories as salaries, payroll taxes and other operating expenses. In the case of income tax expense, we first had to calculate the payable portion and then the cash outlay. For most other expenses involving an accural, the entire expense shown on the income statement is payable. So we can go directly to the formula.

The nature and scope of accrued expenses deserve further comment. To begin, they are frequently referred to as liabilities that change automatically with sales. What that means is that when sales increase, the expenses creating the accrued expenses and hence the liabilities increase. For example, suppose a firm has labor expense of $100 per month and 25% of this is paid in the next month. Accrued expenses at the end of any month will be $25. If sales double, we would expect labor expense to increase. Hence the liability would be larger.

There is an important difference between the way receivables and accrued expenses change with sales. First, as sales change it is likely that receivables will change by approximately the same percentage; that is, if net sales increase 10% it would not be unusual for receivables to increase 10% also. While this direct correspondence with sales could occur with accrued expenses, it is less likely to happen than with receivables because many of the expenses that create accrued liabilities do not change in the same proportion to sales.

Accrued expenses are often referred to as a permanent source of funds. What is meant by this is that although the liability will be paid, it will be recreated continuously. Let's return to our example where labor expense is $100 per month, but 25% of the expense is paid in the next month. Each month the firm will pay $25 from the previous month. However, at the end of any month there will be an accrued expense, a source, of $25 on the firm's balance sheet.

Accrued expenses represents a large percentage of liabilities for many firms. Thus it is considered an important source of funds. While this is true, it is important to realize that this source is fundamentally different from other sources. When a firm borrows from a bank or issues common stock, for example, cash flows into the firm. An accrued expense is not the same type of source—cash does not flow into the firm. Rather, it represents the postponement of paying for an expense. However, it is justifiably considered an important source in the sense that if it did not exist it would have to be replaced by another source. Let's consider an example where labor expense for the month and accrued labor expense at the end of each month are $100 and $25, respectively. If there was not this accrued expense, the firm would need another source and the type of source required would be a permanent one.

So far we have looked at cash inflows from sales and cash outflows related to depreciation, labor expenses and income taxes. Cash outflows related to all expenses except cost of goods sold, can be treated as we treated these three items. Certain expenses are noncash expenses and do not enter the calculations. For all other categories, cash payment and expense recognition might or might not occur in the same period. If the time periods differ, this fact will be signalled by the existence of a prepaid expense and/or an accrued liability.

Let us now turn our attention to cost of goods sold. The chapters on financial accounting discuss cost of goods sold expense and illustrate how it is calculated for a manufacturing business and for a firm that purchases products ready for sale. The two calculations follow.

Manufacturing firm
Beginning inventory of finished goods
+ Cost of goods manufactured
− Ending inventory of finished goods
= Cost of goods sold expense

Firm purchasing products ready for sale
Beginning inventory
+ Purchases
− Ending inventory
= Cost of goods sold expense

For a manufacturing firm we are concerned with cash outlays for manufacturing costs incurred during the period. For the other type of firm we are concerned with cash outlays for purchases. We will deal with the second type only because the difference between the two is a matter of detail—the substance is the same.

The Clinto Company purchases products ready for sale. Therefore, to compute cash outlays related to cost of goods sold expense, we first calculate purchases and then payments for purchases. Both calculations are made for the same period. Using the above formula, we can derive purchases for Clinto for Year 2.

Beginning inventory	$160,000
+ Purchases	?
− Ending inventory	320,000
= Cost of goods sold expense	$3,840,000

Since we know three of the four items in the equation we can derive the fourth, purchases. It comes to $4 million. With this information we can figure out payments for purchases.

The accounts payable (trade account) represents amounts due for purchases. The balance of $160,000 at the end of Year 2 indicates that $3,840,000 of Year 2's purchases of $4 million were paid for during Year 2. The end of Year 1 balance of $80,000 most likely represents purchases made during Year 1 that will be paid in Year 2. Therefore, payments for purchases during Year 2 were $3,920,000. An easier way of computing this is to rely on the following formula:

Accounts payable—trade balance, beginning of period
+ Purchases made during the period
− Accounts payable—trade balance, end of period
= Payments for purchases during period.

For Clinto for Year 2 we have the following:

Accounts payable—trade, end of Year 1	$80,000
+ Purchases	4,000,000
− Accounts payable—trade, end of Year 2	160,000
Payments for purchases during Year 2	$3,920,000

We will say more about payments connected with cost of goods sold expense shortly, but since we have completed the cash inflows and cash outflows, let's summarize them.

Clinto Company—Cash flow from operations for Year 2	
Cash inflows from sales	$4,400,000
− Payments for labor	480,000
− Payments for income taxes	82,000
− Payments for purchases	3,920,000
= (Net) Cash flow from operations	$−82,000

The estimating procedure is designed to give the same amount as shown below.

Net working capital from operations for Year 2	$380,000
− Increase in accounts receivable	400,000
− Increase in inventory	160,000
+ Increase in accounts payable	80,000
+ Increase in accrued taxes	18,000
= Cash flow from operations	$−82,000

The adjustments for changes in inventory and accounts payable both relate to payments connected with cost of goods sold expense, and both deserve further comment.

Inventory must be maintained to support sales; to increase sales requires more inventory. Thus inventory is another asset which normally moves in the same direction as sales. It is difficult to provide a guide for inventory because sometimes it will change in roughly the same proportion as sales, while other times it will change at a slower or more rapid rate. In any case, for many firms, inventory is a substantial dollar amount, and the sales induced changes will represent large sources or uses.

When thinking about the distinction among the flows of net income, net working capital, and cash from operations, it is perhaps best to consider inventory. A large portion of a firm's net income and net working capital generated might be sitting in the increased inventory required to support a higher level of sales. Creditors want payment in cash, not in inventory.

An accounts payable (trade) balance exists when a firm does not have to pay cash or pay in advance for purchases. The size of the account is a function of the level of purchases and credit terms. For example, if purchases are $50 per month and terms are net 30 days, the payable balance will be $50 at the end of each month. If purchases increase to $100 per month and terms stay at net 30 days, then payables will increase to $100. Since purchases are a function of inventory requirements, which are a function of sales, we would expect purchases to change with sales.

Payables to suppliers are similar to accrued expenses in the sense that although payments are made regularly, they are continuously recreated. They represent an important source, very often much larger than accrued expenses. Finally, although cash does not flow into the firm from this source, inventory does and if accounts payable did not support this use, the firm would need an alternative source.

We have now completed our discussion of cash flow from operations. Let us now briefly consider the widely-used technique of adding depreciation expense to net income.

Net income + Depreciation = ?

Many people add depreciation expense to net income and call the sum cash flow from operations. Moreover, they refer to depreciation as a source of funds. Depreciation expense is not a source of funds and the sum of depreciation and net income is an estimate of net working capital from operations, not cash flow.

With respect to depreciation being referred to incorrectly as a source of funds, we most frequently encounter this error in the financial press in quotations made by executives and business writers. These people are not naive or dumb. What they are is careless in their use of words. When they talk about depreciation being a source of funds they are referring to the tax shield created by depreciation. A tax shield is defined as a reduction in the dollars of taxes that must be paid because of an expense. It is calculated as follows: Tax rate × Expense = Tax shield.

To be precise, what they really mean is the following: Revenue is the only source of funds from operating a business. A portion of this source must be used to pay taxes. Depreciation like all deductible expenses has the effect of reducing the portion that must be used to pay taxes. Therefore, if the tax law permits us to increase our depreciation expense, we will be left with a greater portion of our revenues.

People refer to net income plus depreciation as cash flow for two reasons. First, they are being careless in the use of words. What they often mean is that net income plus depreciation is an estimate of cash flow before the impact of changes in net working capital are considered. Second, sometimes net income plus depreciation will provide a decent estimate of cash flow from operations. It is hard to specify the circumstance in which this will be true. A rough rule of thumb calls for the following two conditions: (1) depreciation expense is the only substantial expense that does not reduce net working capital; (2) sales do not change and hence the net working capital items that are automatically affected by sales do not change.

A good analyst will apply this rule properly. The analyst will quickly scan the balance sheet and if a large amount of intangibles is present or if there is a large change in the deferred taxes account, then the rule will not be applied. Further, if the analyst sees that sales have changed by a substantial amount, the rule will not be applied.

Although this rule might have been useful at one time, I would guess that today the opportunities to apply it are relatively rare. Accelerated methods of depreciation and other liberal tax policies have increased the frequency of the use of different accounting policies for financial accounting and tax purposes. As a result, deferred taxes accounts are now quite common on a firm's balance sheet. Moreover, the net working capital accounts are not affected by the number of units sold; rather it is the dollar level of sales that affects them. Even if a firm sells the same number of units, inflation will affect the dollar level and therefore net working capital.

The importance of inflation must not be underestimated. Many people refer to the illusion created by inflation on a firm's reported results. What they are normally talking about is that when we consider the change of the dollar's purchasing power or the replacement cost of inventories and fixed assets the firm's real profits are not nearly as great as reported profits. However, the inflationary impact on sales causes net working capital to increase and this increment must be financed. Putting it more bluntly, the impact of inflation on a firm's financial requirements is very real.

The process of adding depreciation expense to net income is an example of a "rule of thumb" or a "quick and dirty" calculation. As you know, there is a good reason for relying on these. Financial statement analysis and other types of financial analyses take time. Frequently, analysts and managers just do not have the time to perform in-depth analyses and must rely on an approach that is simple. Since these rules are not precise, it is easy to poke holes in them. Perhaps we would all be less critical if we keep in mind that they are designed to give useful approximations, not exact answers. However, we must also be aware that the nature of these rules is such that a certain kind of environment is assumed. When the environment changes, the usefulness of simplified rules might also change.

In closing, since the issue of time constraints was raised, I should address a question that might be in some of your minds. "If I don't have the time to do the analysis I am doing now, where do I find the time to do what this guy recommends?" Notice that applying flow of funds analysis is more a matter of understanding concepts than taking time to push numbers. If your customers already prepare these statements, the only additional pencil pushing might be the calculation of cash flow. Even if they do not, you will find that once you gain some experience, it will take very little time to construct a flow of funds statement.

5

Concluding Comments and References

Most readers of this book fall into one of the three following catagories:

1. Your customers issue income statements, balance sheets, and flow of funds statements prepared according to generally accepted accounting principles (GAAP).
2. Your customers issue GAAP income statements and balance sheets but not flow of funds statements.
3. Your customers use the cash basis of accounting for financial reporting purposes or do not issue statements at all.

Those in category 1 can benefit almost immediately from the topics covered in this book. You should find that once you have mastered the concepts, your financial analysis will take no more time and perhaps less. More importantly, you will see that investing the time to learn the concepts well can have a substantial payoff.

Those of you in category 2 will have to take the time to construct flow of funds statements. Once you gain practice by doing problems like those in Appendix C, you will see that little additional numerical effort is involved. However, it will take time.

Most of us are reluctant to try something new even if we realize it would help. Nonetheless, sometimes something is so important we just can't ignore it. I believe that flow of funds analysis falls into this category, especially for credit managers. In my view when we make decisions based solely or primarily on financial statement analysis we are on shaky ground because such analysis leads to questions and hints at answers, but it does not provide the answers themselves. Unfortunately, sometimes decisions must be made this way. If so, adding flow of funds analysis to ratio analysis makes the ground much less shaky.

Most of you (hopefully) do not fall into category three. Frankly, for those who do, I am not sure what advice to give other than to say that in cash accounting (or no accounting) the risk of extending credit is increased. Keep in mind that profit, properly measured, determines economic viability over time. The statements you receive shorten considerably the time frame over which you can make predictions—if you can make them at all. Consequently, you likely will have to perform analysis more frequently than your more fortunate colleagues.

I should add that if at all possible, you should encourage your customers to prepare income statements, balance sheets, and flow of funds statements according to generally accepted accounting principles. This would benefit them much more than it would help you.

References

The rules governing the preparation of financial statements are continuously reviewed and revisions are not uncommon. Therefore, you will have to keep abreast of changes. Fortunately, business periodicals like the *Wall Street Journal, Business Week,* and *Forbes* are quite useful for this purpose. Also, many of the large public accounting firms issue booklets and newsletters describing contemplated and actual revisions. Perhaps, your accounting department receives them already or could obtain them for you. If so, you should have these publications circulated to your department.

One of the goals of this book is to serve as a useful reference. Hopefully, this goal was achieved. However, it was beyond our scope to cover all accounting rules or to cover all facets of an issue. Therefore, you might have to rely on references. A short list is provided below.

Before turning to these, I will close by noting that I would appreciate receiving any comments or suggestions you might have about the content or style of this book. My address is: Boston College, Department of Finance, Chestnut Hill, Massachusetts 02167.

Accounting references

The following is a list of books I go to when I have questions. By the time you read this book, several will likely be in new editions and so I will not cite the edition.

1. *Accounting: the Language of Business* by Davidson, Schindler, Stickney, and Weil (Horton Company). It contains a comprehensive glossary and other interesting features.

2. *Fundamentals of Financial Accounting* by Anthony and Welsch (Irwin). This is an introductory text.
3. *Intermediate Accounting* by Meigs, Mosich, and Johnson (McGraw-Hill). This is a textbook for courses above the introductory level.
4. *Intermediate Accounting* by Welsch, Zlatkovich, and White (Irwin). This is a textbook for courses above the introductory level.
5. *Financial Statement Analysis: Theory Application and Interpretation* by Bernstein (Irwin). This is a comprehensive treatment of the subject.

Finance references

The two references cited cover more than just financial statement analysis. Topics like cash flow forecasting and present value are included.

1. *Techniques of Financial Analysis* by Helfert (Irwin). This well-known book has been used successfully by many managers. The author is concise and to the point and I think you will find it to be a useful desk reference.
2. *Financial Analysis: Principles and Procedures* by Jerry A. Viscione (Houghton Mifflin Company). You know this author already.

Appendixes

Appendix A—Glossary of accounting terms
Appendix B—Glossary of financial ratios
Appendix C—Examples
Appendix D—Solutions

Appendix A—Glossary of Accounting Terms

This appendix provides a brief explanation of selected accounting terms and account titles not covered in Chapters 1 and 2. The account titles taken directly from annual and 10–K reports are listed here in alphabetical order.

Allowance for unrealized losses on noncurrent marketable equity securities

A contra-asset account, also known as a valuation account, which reports the decrease in the market value of equity securities. This type of account is sometimes shown on the balance sheet when the firm applies the lower of cost or market rule to inventory and/or marketable securities, enabling the reader to see both the original cost of the asset and the decrease in its market value.

Banker's acceptance

This is a short-term debt instrument employed in the financing of foreign trade. Payment is guaranteed by a bank. Often these acceptances are negotiable and readily marketable and many firms include them in their portfolios of marketable securities.

Capital expenditures

These are costs incurred to purchase a new asset or alter an existing asset which will benefit more than one accounting period. The phrase most often refers to expenditures for property, plant, equipment and other fixed assets.

Capital gain

The proceeds from the sale of a capital asset in excess of its book value. If certain conditions are met, part or all of the gain receives preferential tax treatment.

Carryback-carryforward provision of tax laws

A corporation which incurs an operating loss may use the loss to offset income earned in the preceding three years and the subsequent seven years. For example, Firm A incurred a loss of $1,100 in 1981 and its taxable income was $100 in each of the three previous years. The firm would obtain a refund for taxes paid during those three years. Moreover, since only $300 of the $1,100 loss was used to offset prior income, the remaining $800 can be used to offset income for the next seven years.

Cash dividends declared

Dividends which have been announced by the firm's board of directors but have not yet been paid. Once declared, the amount is a legal obligation irrevocable except by the unanimous consent of stockholders and hence is reported as a liability on the firm's books.

Certificates of deposit

These are interest earning bank deposits, often maturing within one year. Larger certificates, typically $100,000 or more, are often negotiable and readily marketable. Many firms include negotiable certificates in their portfolios of marketable securities.

Compensating balances

Demand deposits that a firm must maintain to satisfy the requirements of a loan arrangement and/or to pay the bank for other services. For example, if a firm borrows $100,000 and the compensating balance requirement is 20%, the firm must maintain a balance in its checking account of at least $20,000. If the firm does not normally maintain this amount, then the effective interest rate is higher than the stated rate.

Convertible bonds

A long-term debt instrument which gives the holder the right to exchange it for a specified amount of another security, usually common stock. A convertible bond normally includes a call feature which means that the firm can retire the debt prior to maturity at a stated price. If the market price of the bond is above the call price, the firm has the opportunity to force holders to convert.

Convertible preferred stock

As explained in the second chapter, preferred stock is a financial instrument which normally promises its holders a fixed dividend return. Convertible means that the preferred stock may be exchanged for a stated amount of another security, normally common stock. This security, like convertible bonds discussed above, often contains a call feature.

Copyright

An intangible asset which gives the holder exclusive right to publish and sell a piece of literature or art. The cost of the asset is allocated over the economic life of the copyrighted work.

Current maturities of long-term debt

The portion of the principal of the firm's long-term debt that is due within one year from the balance sheet date.

Deferred charges

An asset representing costs incurred but not yet recorded as an expense. Expense recognition will occur in subsequent accounting periods. This procedure is followed so that the expenditures can be matched with the revenue they help generate.

Deferred compensation

A liability representing expenses incurred for various employee benefit plans such as retirement and vacation plans. Often the liability represents an estimate of what future payments will be.

Deferred employee benefit plan accruals

See deferred compensation

Deferred financing expense

An asset title sometimes used to report the capitalization of interest. Depending on the situation, interest on debt will be recorded as an expense, or recorded as an asset and then charged as an expense in subsequent accounting periods. The accounting profession provides guidelines to help the firm select the appropriate reporting procedure. (The purpose of capitalizing interest expense—recording it as an asset—is to provide better matching of the cost with the revenues that it will help generate.)

Depletion expense

An allocation of the cost of a wasting asset like a mine.

Directors' fees

An expense representing fees paid to members of the firm's board of directors for services rendered.

Dividends payable

A short-term liability that arises when a firm has declared a dividend but has not paid it as of the balance sheet date.

Effective tax rate

Because certain sources of income are nontaxable and certain expenses are not tax deductible, the firm's income tax rate may differ from the statutory rate. Effective tax rate refers to the actual percentage.

Excess of replacement value of insurance proceeds over net book value on equipment loss

Income statement item which represents other income, that is, income from a source other than normal continuing operations. This specific account indicates that the insurance proceeds exceeded the carrying value of the asset on the firm's books.

Foreign exchange losses—net

An expense which recognizes the net effect of changes in the various currencies in which the firm transacts business.

Franchise

A right to operate under a specific name and/or to sell certain goods or services.

Interest capitalized

See deferred financing expense.

Inventory on consignment

An asset which represents goods shipped by a firm to another party for approval and/or to act as a sales agent. Even though the firm no longer has possession, it still has title and owns the goods until a transaction occurs.

Investments in and advances to wholly-owned subsidiaries

An asset indicating the parent's equity in a subsidiary. When such an asset appears on a firm's consolidated balance sheet, it means that the financial statements of one or more subsidiaries are not included. (See discussion of investments account in Chapter 2 for further explanation.)

Investment tax credit

A reduction in taxes which is the result of expenditures on certain kinds of long-lived assets. The amount is a percentage of the cost of the assets. On a firm's income statement, the credit will be recognized as a reduction in income tax expense either in the year it is granted or it will be spread out over the life of the asset.

Lease

An arrangement giving the lessee the right to use an asset for a specified period of time. The terms of the lease agreement dictates the accounting treatment. In some cases, lease payments will be recorded as an expense for the period. In other cases, the present value of the future lease payments will be recorded as an asset and a liability on the leasee's books even though the property is not owned. In the latter instance, the cost of the asset is allocated as an expense over subsequent accounting periods and the liability is also reduced as payments are made. Note that this description refers to the financial accounting treatment, not the tax treatment.

Leasehold improvements

An intangible asset which reflects expenditures made to leased property. The cost is charged as an expense over subsequent accounting periods.

Line of credit

An informal short-term loan arrangement giving the borrower the opportunity to obtain funds up to a certain limit for a specified period of time. Lines of credit are frequently used to finance a firm's seasonal borrowing requirements.

Minority interest in net assets of consolidated subsidiary

When a firm does not own 100% of a subsidiary whose financial statements are included in the consolidated statements, the ownership of other parties is reported as minority interest. It will be classified as a liability or included in the stockholders' equity section.

Mortgage debt

Long-term debt secured by real property, normally land and/or buildings.

Patent

An asset representing a right to a process for a specific period of time. It appears on a firm's balance sheet when it has been purchased and the asset is amortized over the shorter of the legal life of the patent or the useful life of the process. Costs incurred by the firm to develop a patent internally must be expensed in the period that the costs are incurred.

Provision for disposition and termination of operations

A liability representing anticipated costs that will be incurred in the future as the result of the termination of operations.

Provision for obsolescence of inventory

An expense representing the estimated decline in the value of inventory due to obsolescence.

Purchase deposits with manufacturers of equipment

A fixed asset account representing initial downpayments on equipment to be received in the future.

Redeemable preferred stock

Preferred stock with a provision which allows or requires the firm to retire the stock under certain specified terms. Redeemable preferred cannot be classified as part of stockholders' equity. (Current rules require that redeemable preferred be separately classified and consideration is being given to treating it as a liability.)

Registered securities

Most firms selling securities to the public must register them with the Securities and Exchange Commission. The registration statement includes information about the company.

Repurchase agreement

An arrangement where one party purchases securities, usually short-term debt instruments, from another party and the seller agrees to buy them back from the purchaser on a certain date and at an agreed upon price.

Revolving credit arrangement

Borrowing agreement where the creditor agrees to lend up to a certain amount for a specified period of time. Unlike a line of credit which is described above, this is a formal agreement and the lender is legally committed to supply funds. Moreover, whereas a line of credit is a short-term arrangement, this one often runs for a three to five year period.

Serial bond

A long-term liability where portions of the principal are due at different dates. In other words, there is a series of maturity dates.

Sinking fund debt

When a long-term debt issue contains a sinking fund provision, this indicates that payments are required prior to maturity. Usually the payments are used to retire a portion of the debt and this part is no longer an obligation of the firm.

Stock dividend

Dividends issued in additional shares of stock. It is recognized on the firm's books by transferring a portion of the retained earnings balance to the common stock and paid-in capital accounts.

Stock option

The holder of the option has the right to purchase shares of stock at a stated price for a specified period of time. They are most often granted to employees and managers to motivate them to act in the best interest of the firm's shareholders.

Stock split

A stock split is a change in the number of common shares outstanding. For example, a 2 for 1 split means each shareholder now has twice as many shares. The only adjustment on the firm's books is a change in the par or stated value of the stock.

Stock warrant

An option to purchase a specified number of shares of stock at a given price for a stated period of time.

Time deposit

Money in a bank or thrift institution which earns interest. On a firm's balance sheet this asset may be separately classified or included with cash or marketable securities.

Trademark

The right to employ a certain name or certain words in advertisements. It appears on the balance sheet as an asset when the right has been purchased and is normally written off over a certain period of time. Costs incurred by a firm to develop a trademark internally must be expensed in the period that the costs are incurred.

Wasting asset

An asset such as a natural resource (e.g. oil, timber, natural gas) which is subject to being used up and/or must be further developed to be of use in the future.

Appendix B—Glossary of Financial Ratios

This appendix presents a list of ratios organized into the following four catagories:

Liquidity. These help to evaluate the ability of a firm to pay its current liabilities as they come due.

Financial Leverage or Solvency. These ratios measure the extent to which a firm relies on debt financing.

Activity or Efficiency. These provide insight into how well a firm is controlling and managing its assets and current liabilities.

Profitability. Ratios included in this category are designed to help the analyst evaluate a firm's ability to control expenses and to earn a return on the economic resources committed to the business.

No taxonomy for ratios is perfect and other authors would rely on a different classification. Moreover, they might not agree with my selection of ratios for each category. For example, I include the days purchases outstanding ratio in the activity category; others might prefer to include it in the liquidity category.

Each ratio is preceded by a brief explanation of its purposes. I hesitated to include such descriptions because they can be misleading. Ratios provide clues and insights into a firm's financial health and performance. They do not enable one to reach firm conclusions; rather, ratios are most useful as a starting point for further analysis because they help the analyst to ask the right kinds of questions and to pinpoint certain areas that require further attention.

LIQUIDITY RATIOS

1. Current ratio—a measure of a firm's ability to pay its short-term liabilities.

$$\text{Current ratio} = \frac{\text{Current assets}}{\text{Current liabilities}}$$

2. Acid test or Quick ratio—designed to be a more rigid test (than the current ratio) of a firm's ability to pay its current liabilities. Two versions exist and the first is recommended by the author.

Version 1

$$\text{Acid test} = \frac{\text{Cash} + \text{Marketable securities} + \text{Accounts receivable}}{\text{Current liabilities}}$$

Version 2

$$\text{Acid test} = \frac{\text{Current assets} - \text{Inventory}}{\text{Current liabilities}}$$

3. Liquid asset ratio—considered to be the most rigorous test of a firm's ability to pay its current liabilities.

$$\text{Liquid asset ratio} = \frac{\text{Cash} + \text{Marketable securities}}{\text{Current liabilities}}$$

4. Defensive interval—estimate of how long a firm can meet expected expenditures without relying on inflows of liquid assets. Various measures are used, two common versions are:

Version 1

$$\text{Defensive interval} = \frac{\text{Cash} + \text{Marketable securities}}{\text{Projected daily expenditures}}$$

Version 2

$$\text{Defensive interval} = \frac{\text{Cash} + \text{Marketable securities} + \text{Accounts receivable}}{\text{Projected daily expenditures}}$$

5. Funds flow measure—an estimate of how long it will take operations to generate the funds necessary to pay current liabilities. Usually, analysts rely on the previous year's level for an estimate. Various versions are possible; two are:

Version 1

$$\text{Funds flow measure} = \frac{\text{Current liabilities} - (\text{Cash} + \text{Market security} + \text{Accounts receivables})}{\text{Annual net working capital from operations}} \times 360 \text{ days}$$

Version 2

$$\text{Funds flow measure} = \frac{\text{Current liabilities}}{\text{Annual net working capital from operations}} \times 360 \text{ days}$$

6. Composition measures—A number of ratios are employed to help the analyst evaluate the liquidity of a firm's assets. Each ratio relates a specific asset or group of assets to either total assets, total current assets or net working capital.

FINANCIAL LEVERAGE OR SOLVENCY RATIOS

1. Debt to asset ratio—measures the proportion of a firm's assets financed by debt.

$$\text{Debt to asset ratio} = \frac{\text{Total debt}}{\text{Total assets}}$$

2. Equity to asset ratio—like the preceding ratio, it measures the proportion of a firm's assets financed by debt.

$$\text{Equity to asset ratio} = \frac{\text{Owners' equity}}{\text{Total assets}}$$

3. Debt to equity ratio—measures how many dollars of debt are being employed for each dollar of equity. Various versions are employed; two are:

Version 1

$$\text{Total debt to equity} = \frac{\text{Total liabilities}}{\text{Owners' equity}}$$

Version 2

$$\text{Long-term debt to equity} = \frac{\text{Long-term debt}}{\text{Owners' equity}}$$

4. Capitalization ratio—measures the proportion of a firm's permanent capital that is financed with debt.

$$\text{Capitalization ratio} = \frac{\text{Long-term debt}}{\text{Long-term debt} + \text{Owners' equity}}$$

5. Interest coverage ratio—helps to evaluate the firm's ability to meet required interest payments.

$$\text{Interest coverage} = \frac{\text{Profit before deducting interest and taxes}}{\text{Interest expense}}$$

6. Fixed charge coverage—helps to evaluate the firm's ability to meet interest and lease payments. (Other fixed obligations might also be included.)

$$\text{Fixed charge coverage} = \frac{\text{Profit before deducting interest, lease payments and taxes}}{\text{Interest expense} + \text{Lease payments}}$$

7. Burden coverage—helps to evaluate the firm's ability to meet principal payments on debt as well as interest and lease payments.

$$\text{Burden coverage} = \frac{\text{Profit before deducting interest, lease payments and taxes}}{\text{Interest expense} + \text{Lease payments} + \dfrac{\text{Principal payments}}{1 - \text{Tax rate}}}$$

8. Long-term debt to net working capital ratio—helps to evaluate a firm's ability to pay its long-term debt from current assets after providing for current liabilities.

$$\text{Long-term debt to net working capital} = \frac{\text{Long-term debt}}{\text{Current assets} - \text{Current liabilities}}$$

9. Funds flow statement ratios—Various measures are used to relate information from the firm's funds flow statement to some facet of its debt. These ratios are designed to provide insight into a firm's ability to generate the cash from operations to cover required debt payments. One example is to relate cash flow to principal payments on long-term debt due within one year as shown below.

$$\frac{\text{Cash flow from operations}}{\text{Current maturities of long-term debt}}$$

ACTIVITY OR EFFICIENCY RATIOS

1. Total asset turnover—provides insight into how well a firm's assets are controlled and managed by measuring how many

dollars of sales can be generated with each dollar of assets. (Sometimes an average of assets at various points in the year is used in the denominator.)

$$\text{Total asset turnover} = \frac{\text{Net sales}}{\text{Total assets}}$$

2. Accounts receivable turnover—helps to evaluate if a change in receivables is due to sales or to some other factor such as a lengthening of the collection period. (Sometimes credit sales is the numerator and an average of accounts receivable at various points in the year is the denominator.)

$$\text{Accounts receivable turnover} = \frac{\text{Net sales}}{\text{Accounts receivable}}$$

3. Days sales outstanding ratio—this measure, also known as the average collection period, helps to evaluate how quickly a firm collects its receivables.

$$\text{Days sales outstanding} = \frac{\text{Accounts receivable}}{\dfrac{\text{Net sales}}{\text{360 days}}}$$

The formula advocated by the Credit Research Foundation, the National Association of Credit Management's educational arm is as follows:

$$\text{Days sales outstanding} = \frac{\text{Average trade receivables balance last 3 month-ends} \times 90}{\text{Credit sales for the last 3 months}}$$

Note: Credit analysts rely on this ratio a great deal. However, it is at best a rough guide and only under very specific conditions will it provide an accurate portrayal of how long it takes a firm to collect its receivables.

4. Inventory turnover—helps to evaluate how well a firm controls and manages its inventory by estimating how long on average it takes a firm to sell its inventory. (In the two versions that follow ending inventory is the denominator; sometimes an average of inventory at various points in the year is the denominator.)

Version 1

$$\text{Inventory turnover} = \frac{\text{Net sales}}{\text{Ending inventory}}$$

Version 2

$$\text{Inventory turnover} = \frac{\text{Cost of goods sold}}{\text{Ending inventory}}$$

5. Net working capital turnover—provides insight into how effectively net working capital is being employed.

$$\text{Net working capital turnover} = \frac{\text{Net sales}}{\text{Current assets} - \text{Current liabilities}}$$

6. Days purchases outstanding ratio—helps to evaluate if a firm pays its trade payables on time. (Sometimes a period shorter than one year is used to calculate average daily purchases. Moreover, if the firm purchases some of its goods for cash, only credit purchases should be included if that information is available.)

$$\text{Days purchases outstanding} = \frac{\text{Accounts payable}}{\frac{\text{Purchases}}{\text{360 days}}}$$

7. Fixed asset turnover—a measure used by analysts to evaluate capacity utilization and the quality of the firm's fixed assets. For example, a low turnover might be a sign of excess capacity and a high rate might mean that the firm is relying on old plant and equipment.

$$\text{Fixed asset turnover} = \frac{\text{Net sales}}{\text{Net fixed assets}}$$

8. Cash turnover—helps to evaluate how well a firm is utilizing its cash balances; marketable securities might be included in the denominator.

$$\text{Cash turnover} = \frac{\text{Net sales}}{\text{Cash}}$$

PROFITABILITY RATIOS

1. Net profit margin—measures the income earned on each dollar of sales; can be calculated on a pre-tax or after-tax basis.

After-Tax Basis

$$\frac{\text{Net income after taxes}}{\text{Net sales}}$$

Before-Tax Basis

$$\frac{\text{Net income before taxes}}{\text{Net sales}}$$

2. 100% statements—net sales is set equal to 100% and each expense category is stated as a percentage of sales. This is done by dividing each expense by the net sales figure. These statements help to evaluate how successful the firm has been in controlling expenses and to explain changes in the firm's net profit margin. An example follows.

Net sales	$1,000	100%
Cost of goods sold	400	40%
Selling expenses	200	20%
Administrative expenses	100	10%
Profit before taxes	$300	30%
Income taxes	150	15%
Net income	$ 150	15%

3. Gross margin rate—measures how profitable sales are when only the cost of the products (or services) sold is considered.

$$\text{Gross profit rate} = \frac{\text{Net sales} - \text{Cost of goods sold}}{\text{Net sales}}$$

4. Return on assets—This ratio, also known as the DuPont formula, provides insight into the firm's overall profitability. Various measures are used and we will show three of them. (Sometimes, an average of assets at different points in the year is the denominator.)

Version 1

$$\text{Return on assets} = \frac{\text{Net income after taxes}}{\text{Total assets}}$$

Note: This ratio can be stated as follows:

$$\frac{\text{Net income after taxes}}{\text{Total assets}} = \frac{\text{Net income after taxes}}{\text{Net sales}} \times \frac{\text{Net sales}}{\text{Total assets}}$$

This restatement illustrates that overall profitability depends on both the profitability of each sales dollar and the efficient employment of assets.

Version 2

$$\text{Return on assets} = \frac{\text{Net income after taxes} + \text{Interest expense}}{\text{Total assets}}$$

Version 3

$$\text{Return on assets} = \frac{\text{Profit before deducting interest and taxes}}{\text{Total assets}}$$

5. Return on equity—measures the return on the owners' investment. (Sometimes an average of net worth at different points in the year is the denominator.)

$$\text{Return on equity} = \frac{\text{Net income after taxes}}{\text{Owners' equity}}$$

Note: This ratio can be stated as follows:

$$\frac{\text{Net income after taxes}}{\text{Owners' equity}} = \frac{\text{Net income after taxes}}{\text{Net sales}} \times \frac{\text{Net sales}}{\text{Total assets}} \times \frac{\text{Total assets}}{\text{Owner's equity}}$$

This restatement illustrates that return on equity depends on profitability of sales, asset efficiency, and financial leverage.

6. Return on common equity—if a firm has preferred stock outstanding, focus might be placed on common equity by making the following adjustment to the preceding ratio.

$$\text{Return on common equity} = \frac{\text{Net income after taxes} - \text{Preferred dividend}}{\text{Owners' equity} - \text{Preferred stock}}$$

7. Contribution margin rate—measures the proportion of each sales dollar that is available for fixed costs and profits.

$$\text{Contribution margin rate} = \frac{\text{Net sales} - \text{Variable expense}}{\text{Net sales}}$$

8. Price earnings ratio—indicates the price investors are willing to pay for each dollar of earning.

$$\text{Price earnings ratio} = \frac{\text{Market price per share of common stock}}{\text{Earnings per share}}$$

9. Price/book ratio—traditionally used as a measure of risk involved in investing in a firm's common stock. Now more popular as a measure to identify potential acquisition candidates.

$$\text{Price/book ratio} = \frac{\text{Market price per share of common stock}}{\text{Book value per share of common stock}}$$

Appendix C—Examples

This appendix presents nine examples designed to give you practice in learning how to construct flow of funds statements. The first four call for verbal responses and numerical calculations are required for the last five. Suggested solutions follow in Appendix D. Please note that the purpose of the appendix will be defeated if you refer too quickly to the solutions. If you encounter difficulty, you should spend a reasonable amount of time trying to resolve it before looking to the answer.

Example 1

If the word "funds" appears on a flow of funds statement, what does it mean?

Example 2

Assume that in the long-term asset section of a balance sheet you find a deferred taxes account. How would you treat changes in this asset on a flow of funds statement?

Example 3

Sometimes deferred taxes will be a current liability or a current asset. How are changes in these accounts treated in a flow of funds analysis?

Example 4

How is a net loss treated on a flow of funds statement?

Example 5

You are given the following information for the Seldo Company.

Income Statements
Years Ending December 31

	1980	1981
Net sales	$ 3,500	$ 4,700
Cost of goods sold	2,500	2,900
Gross margin	$ 1,000	$ 1,800
Selling, general and administrative*	400	600
Income before taxes	$ 600	$ 1,200
Income tax expense	150	240
Net Income	$ 450	$ 960
Dividends	$ 430	$ 945

*includes depreciation expense of $200 in 1980 and $300 for 1981.

Balance Sheets

	at 12/31/1980	at 12/31/1981
Cash	$ 50	$ 70
Accounts receivable	200	240
Inventory	300	330
Total current	$ 550	$ 640
Property, plant and equipment—net	1,430	1,440
Total assets	$ 1,980	$ 2,080
Accounts payable—trade	$ 300	$ 310
Short-term bank loan	20	25
Accrued income taxes	40	60
Total current	$ 360	$ 395
Common stock	100	110
Capital surplus	500	540
Retained earnings	1,020	1,035
Total	$ 1,980	$ 2,080

Prepare a flow of funds statement for the year ended December 31, 1981.

Example 6

You are given the following information for the Gilder Company.

Balance sheets as of December 31, 1978
and December 31, 1982
(000 omitted)

	1978	1982
Cash	$ 800	$ 1,600
Accounts receivable	3,900	5,100
Inventory	2,600	3,900
Net fixed assets	6,000	4,000
Total	$13,300	$14,600
Accounts payable	$ 1,200	$ 2,600
Long-term debt	1,000	200
Deferred taxes (noncurrent)	800	1,400
Common stock	3,300	3,400
Retained earnings	7,000	7,000
Total	$13,300	$14,600

Income statement data (000 omitted)

	Year Ending 12/31/78	Year Ending 12/31/79	Year Ending 12/31/80	Year Ending 12/31/81	Year Ending 12/31/82
Net income after taxes	$16,000	$4,000	$4,000	$2,000	$2,000
Dividends	1,000	1,000	1,000	5,000	5,000
Depreciation expenses	200	200	200	200	200

Prepare a flow of funds statement for the four year period ending December 31, 1982.

Example 7

You are given the following information for the H Company.

Income Statement
Year Ending December 31, 1982
(In $millions)

Net sales	$572.6
Cost of goods sold	431.8
Gross profit	$140.8
Operating expenses	101.7
Income before taxes	$ 39.1
Provision for income taxes	19.0
Net income	$ 20.1
Dividends	$ 9.1

Note: Depreciation expense for the year was $14 million.

Balance Sheets
(In $ millions)

	at 12/31/81	at 12/31/82
Cash	$ 10.0	$ 15.0
Accounts receivable	60.0	70.0
Inventory	82.0	87.3
Net fixed assets	105.7	103.7
Total assets	$257.7	$276.0
Accounts payable	$ 47.5	$ 62.8
Long-term debt	30.4	12.4
Stockholders' equity	179.8	200.8
Total liabilities and stockholders' equity	$257.7	$276.0

Prepare a flow of funds statement for the year ended December 31, 1982.

Example 8

You are given the following information for the Dixfi Company.

Balance Sheets
Years Ending 12/31
(In $ thousands)

	1981	1982
Cash	$ 15	$ 15
Accounts receivable	40	36
Inventories	18	29
Prepaid Expenses	6	13
Total current	$ 79	$ 93
Property, plant and equipment	30	50
less Accumulated depreciation	10	12
Property, plant and equipment—net	20	38
Total assets	$ 99	$131
Accounts payable	$ 11	$ 19
Short-term debt	10	5
Total current	21	24
Deferred income taxes	18	16
Common stock	14	15
Paid-in capital	17	19
Retained earnings	29	57
Total liabilities and owners' equity	$ 99	$131

Income data (in $ thousands)

Net income after taxes	$ 42	$ 56
Dividends	21	28
Depreciation expense	16	17

Prepare a flow of funds statement for the year ended December 31, 1982.

Example 9

You are given the following information.

SUNEL COMPANY
Balance Sheets
As of December 31
(000 omitted)

	1980	1982
Cash	$ 8	$ 5
Marketable securities	14	16
Receivables	23	29
Inventory	46	53
Fixed assets—net	83	87
Total	$174	$190
Accounts payable	$ 41	$ 51
Long-term debt	16	23
Common stock	67	77
Retained earnings	50	39
Total	$174	$190

Income data (000 omitted)

	1980	1981	1982
Net income after taxes	$ 20	($ 21)	$ 20
Dividends	$ 10	0	$ 10
Depreciation	$ 18	$ 19	$ 10

Prepare a flow of funds statement for the two year period ending December, 31, 1982.

Appendix D—Solutions

Suggested Solution to Example 1

It could signify various quantities. It most frequently refers to net working capital, but it could also mean cash, assets, or something else.

Suggested Solution to Example 2

An increase would be subtracted from net income and a decrease would be added in calculating net working capital provided by operations.

Suggested Solution to Example 3

They are not included in the computation of net working capital from operations but they are part of the calculation of cash flow from operations.

Suggested Solution to Example 4

A net loss can be viewed as a negative (profit) number. When depreciation expense is added to it and other appropriate adjustments are made, if the total is still negative it is listed as a use of funds, signifying that operations decreased net working capital. If the total is positive, it would be shown as a source because the positive sum indicates that operations increased net working capital.

Suggested Solution to Example 5

SELDO COMPANY
Flow of Funds Statement
Year Ending December 31, 1981

Sources		
Operations:		
Net income	$ 960	
+ depreciation expenses	300	
Total		$1,260
Accounts payable		10
Short-term bank loan		5
Accrued income taxes		20
Common stock		10
Capital surplus		40
Total		$1,345
Uses		
Dividends		$ 945
Net additions to fixed assets		310
Accounts receivable		40
Inventory		30
Cash		20
Total		$1,345

Suggested Solution to Example 6

GILDER COMPANY
Flow of Funds Statement for Four Year
Period Ending December 31, 1982
(000 omitted)

Sources		
Operations:		
Net income	$12,000	
Deferred income taxes	600	
Depreciation expenses	800	
Total		$13,400
Net proceeds from sale of fixed assets		1,200
Accounts payable		1,400
Common stock		100
Total		$16,100
Uses		
Dividends		$12,000
Accounts receivable		1,200
Inventory		1,300
Long-term debt		800
Cash		800
Total		$16,100

Comments

Some of you might have made the error of including data from the income statement for the year ended December 31, 1978. We are studying the period January 1, 1979, to December 31, 1982, the data from 1978's income statement pertains to a prior period.

Suggested Solution to Example 7

H COMPANY
Flow of Funds Statement
For Year Ending December 31, 1982

Sources		
Funds provided by operations:		
Net income	$20.1	
Depreciation expenses	14.0	$34.1
Common stock		10.0
Accounts payable		15.3
Total		$59.4
Uses		
Dividends		$ 9.1
Net additions to fixed assets		12.0
Accounts receivable		10.0
Inventory		5.3
Long-term debt		18.0
Cash		5.0
Total		$59.4

Comments

1. Net fixed assets decreased by $2 million but when you add depreciation expense of $14 million to this number you get $12 million as the net amount spent.

Change in net fixed assets	−2
+ depreciation expense	14
= Estimate of net amount spent	12

2. Stockholders' equity consists of capital stock accounts and retained earnings. Since net income was $20.1 million and dividends were $9.1 million, then retained earnings likely increased by $11.0 million (unless there was another entry affecting retained earnings). Since the total of stockholders' equity increased by $21 million, the remainder is most likely common stock.

Suggested Solution to Example 8

DIXFI COMPANY
Flow of Funds Statement
Year Ending December 31, 1982
(In $ thousands)

Source		
Funds from Operation:		
Net income	$56	
Depreciation expense	17	
Deferred taxes—noncurrent	(2)	$71
Accounts receivable		4
Accounts payable		8
Common stock		1
Paid-in capital		2
		$86
Uses		
Dividends		$28
Inventory		11
Prepaid expenses		7
Net addition to fixed assets		35
Short-term debt		5
Total		$86

Comments

. On this balance sheet we have the gross fixed asset account and the net amount shown. Some analysts take the change in the gross amount. I used the net figure and I recommend that you follow the rule provided in the book, even when the gross figure is shown; that is, add depreciation expense to the change in next fixed assets.

2. The long-term deferred taxes liability decreased and so it was subtracted from net income to estimate the amount of net working capital provided by operations.

Suggested Solution to Example 9

SUNEL COMPANY
Flow of Funds Statement
For the Two Years Ending December 31, 1982
(000 omitted)

Sources		
Funds flow:		
Net loss	($1)	
+ depreciation	29	$28
Cash		3
Accounts payable		10
Long-term debt		7
Common stock		10
		$58
Uses		
Dividends		$10
Marketable securities		2
Receivables		6
Inventory		7
Net additions to fixed assets		33
Total		$58

Comments

Some of you might have made the error of including data from the income statement for the year ended December 31, 1980. We are studying the period January 1, 1981 to December 31, 1982; the income data for the year ended December 31, 1980 pertains to a prior period.

About the Author

Jerry A. Viscione is a professor of finance at Boston College, where he was recently appointed chairman of the finance department. He has also taught at Harvard University. He received his Ph.D. in economics from Boston University in 1973 and holds degrees in accounting, finance and economics from Boston University and Boston College.

Dr. Viscione is the author of *How to Construct Pro Forma Statements* published by NACM in 1980 and *Financial Analysis: Principles and Procedures* published by the Houghton Mifflin Company in 1977. He is also the co-author of Houghton Mifflin's *Cases in Financial Management.*

His articles on finance have been published in several leading business journals, including *Bell Journal of Economics, Financial Management, The Financial Review, Journal of Financial Education, Real Estate Review, Credit and Financial Management* and *Management Review.*

Dr. Viscoine serves as consultant to various small businesses. He participates on numerous committees at Boston College. He finds time for community services and is active with the Ecumenical Life Center for Elders, United Way and the East Boston-Wellesley College Cooperative Program.

NACM

The National Association of Credit Management is a member-owned and controlled organization of 87 affiliated local associations in the United States and an international subsidiary that operates in Europe. The NACM was founded in 1896 to promote good laws for sound credit; protect business against fraudulent debtors; improve the interchange of credit information; develop better credit practices and methods and establish a code of ethics. In addition to those original objectives, education and research programs illustrate NACM's awareness of the complex needs of credit management today. Membership in an NACM-affiliated credit association includes membership in the National Association of Credit Management. Members of the NACM are credit and financial executives, primarily representing manufacturers, wholesalers, financial institutions and varied service organizations. Membership now exceeds 44,000. For information regarding membership, write to executive offices: 475 Park Avenue South, New York, N.Y. 10016